ZOOM IN ...

Studying and Working Abroad

Herausgegeben von:
Iris Faßbender und Colette Granvillano

Erarbeitet von:
Fenna Campen und Denise Frohn

Schöningh

Acknowledgements

Huber Kartographie, München/Verlagsarchiv Schöningh: U2, U3; © Ekaterina Pokrovsky - Fotolia.com: p. 6 top l.; © pedarilhos - Fotolia.com: p. 6 bottom; © vario images: p. 6 top r.; © Mykola Mazuryk - shutterstock.com: p. 7; © gustavofrazao - Fotolia.com: p. 8; © tomo888 - Fotolia.com: p. 10; © Robert Kneschke - Fotolia.com: p. 15; © picture-alliance/dpa: p. 16, p. 17, p. 45, p. 66, p. 86; © roxx0r - Fotolia.com: p. 19; DAAD/DZHW (Hg.): Wissenschaft Weltoffen 2015. Daten und Fakten zur Internationalität von Studium und Forschung in Deutschland. Bielefeld 2015: p. 20; Franz-Josef Domke, Hannover/Verlagsarchiv Schöningh: p. 22, p. 30 bottom, p. 53, p. 64 bottom; www.CartoonStock.com: p. 23, p. 85 top l.; © Chris Frape: p. 25; © ddp images/CAMERA PRESS/Francesco Guidicini: p. 27; © Black Swan: p. 29; © ddp images: p. 30 top; © UWATX: p. 34 bottom l.; © Fenna Campen: p. 34 top; © BRIGITTE WEIDLICH/AFP/Getty Images: p. 34 bottom r.; © Netfalls - Fotolia.com: p. 37; © Paul Harris/Getty Images: p. 40; Photo by Leah Puttkammer/Getty Images: p. 42; By I, Valio vitanov, CC BY-SA 2.5, https://commons.wikimedia.org/w/index.php?curid=2445642: p. 43 bottom; © Peace Corps: p. 44; © Joel Carillet - iStockphoto.com: p. 47; © OlegD - shutterstock.com: p. 49; © 2007 Warner Bros. Ent., All Rights Reserved: p. 51; © contrastwerkstatt - Fotolia.com: p. 52; © Entrypark: p. 59; © ullstein bild - Thierlein: p. 64 centre; © s4svisuals - Fotolia.com: p. 64 l.; © Johnny Greig - iStockphoto.com: p. 68; www.global-integration.com: p. 71; © picture-alliance/Yonhap: p. 73; © IS_ImageSource - iStockphoto.com: p. 74; © ShadowCatcher Entertainment: p. 76/77; THE CIRCLE by Dave Eggers, copyright © 2013 by Dave Eggers. Used by permission of Alfred A. Knopf, an imprint of the Knopf Doubleday Publishing Group, a division of Random House: p. 79; Copyright © BBC: p. 81 top l./r.; ullstein bild: p. 81 bottom; Wikipedia/The Opte Project: p. 82; ROGERS ©2013 Pittsburgh Post-Gazette. Reprinted by permission of UNIVERSAL UCLICK. All rights reserved.: p. 85 bottom l.; KDnuggets.com - a leading site for Big Data, Data Science and Data Mining: p. 85 top r.; © Matt Wuerker: p. 85 bottom r.; F.A.Z.-Grafik / Felix Brocker: p. 88; others: Verlagsarchiv Schöningh

Muttersprachliche Betreuung: Ronnie Halligan

www.schoeningh-schulbuch.de
Schöningh Verlag, Jühenplatz 1–3, 33098 Paderborn

Druck A 5 4 3 2 1 / Jahr 2020 19 18 17 16
Alle Drucke der Serie A sind im Unterricht parallel verwendbar.
Die letzte Zahl bezeichnet das Jahr dieses Druckes.

Umschlaggestaltung: Reinhild Kassing, Kassel
Umschlagabbildung: © Nomad_Soul/shutterstock
Druck und Bindung: westermann druck GmbH, Braunschweig

ISBN 978-3-14-040660-4

Zur Arbeit mit dem Buch

Anforderungsbereiche

Alle Aufgaben dieses Bandes sind farbig gekennzeichnet und sind somit den drei Anforderungsbereichen eindeutig zuzuordnen. Eine detaillierte Aufstellung aller Operatoren finden Sie im Anhang.

AFB I: Comprehension

AFB II: Analysis

AFB III: Evaluation/Re-creation of text

Aufgaben, die einen Text inhaltlich/sprachlich vorbereiten beziehungsweise weiterführend vertiefen, sind grau unterlegt.

Symbole

Auf verschiedenen Seiten dieses Bandes finden Sie Symbole, die auf sprachlich-methodische Fertigkeiten, Musterlösungen und weiterführende Aktivitäten hinweisen.

Speaking – Mithilfe dieser Aufgabe wird der mündliche Ausdruck geübt.

Listening – Zu diesem Material gibt es im Lehrerband eine Audio-Datei (auf CD), mit der das Hörverstehen geschult wird.

Mediation – Dieses Material wird in eigenen Worten auf Englisch bzw. auf Deutsch wiedergegeben und dient der Sprachmittlung.

Model solution – Zu dieser Aufgabe liegt eine Musterlösung vor.

Activity – Bei dieser Aufgabe werden die Schülerinnen und Schüler in vielfältiger Weise selbst aktiv.

Webcodes

Webcodes verweisen auf Zusatzmaterial im Internet und erleichtern Ihnen das Auffinden von Links und Dateien, die speziell für den vorliegenden Band ausgewählt oder erstellt wurden.

@ SNG-40660-001

Zur Nutzung gehen Sie bitte auf folgende Seite: http://www.schoeningh-schulbuch.de/webcodes

Geben Sie dort den Code ein, um zu dem jeweiligen Material zu gelangen.

Contents

Getting started

Student studying in front of the Eiffel Tower

A high school intern in Detroit, U.S.

Backpacker during her gap year

1902	1914	1 January, 1925	1929	1946	1949	28 July, 1957	25 March, 1957	1 March, 1961
The Rhodes Scholarship is established as a prestigious programme for international scholarships by British colonist Cecil John Rhodes.	The AFS Intercultural Programs, formerly the American Field Service, is a non-profit organisation which offers youth exchanges worldwide.	Foundation of 'DAAD' with the aim of promoting international exchange students, scientists and artists. The programme puts a focus on cultural as well as educational development.	The Rotary Youth Exchange sends their first international students on a cultural and academic exchange in secondary school.	The Fulbright Program is introduced in 1946. The U.S. programme supports students, teachers, scientists and artists in international educational exchanges.	Foundation of AIESEC, which offers international internships and leadership programmes.	The 'Youth for Understanding Committee' (YFU) is established in Germany by young students who had the chance to experience a stay in the US themselves. The programme offers a youth exchange.	Creation of the European Economic Community, first basis of the European Union.	J. F. Kennedy sets up the U.S. Peace Corps, a volunteer programme which has been run by the US government ever since. Its aim is to provide technical, cultural and economic assistance.

"The world is a book and those who do not travel read only one page."
–Augustine of Hippo

"Why do you go away? So that you can come back. So that you can see the place you came from with new eyes and extra colors. And the people there see you differently, too. Coming back to where you started is not the same as never leaving."
–Terry Pratchett

"The real voyage of discovery consists not in seeking new landscapes, but in having new eyes."
–Marcel Proust

"The traveler sees what he sees. The tourist sees what he has come to see."
–G.K. Chesterton

"Travel makes one modest. You see what a tiny place you occupy in the world."
–Gustave Flaubert

"All journeys have secret destinations of which the traveller is unaware."
–Martin Buber

"Perhaps travel cannot prevent bigotry*, but by demonstrating that all peoples cry, laugh, eat, worry, and die, it can introduce the idea that if we try and understand each other, we may even become friends."
–Maya Angelou

bigotry prejudice, discrimination

"The journey, not the arrival matters."
–T.S. Elliot

"To travel is to discover that everyone is wrong about other countries."
–Aldous Huxley

1. Speculate on the thoughts and motivation of the people depicted on the left before and while these pictures were taken.

2. Read the quotes on travelling and staying abroad in order to choose one of them that you can relate to. In a milling around activity, explain to your interlocutors why you have chosen this particular quote.

22 January, 1963	5 July, 1963	1974	15 June, 1987	1 November, 1993	1996	2009	2014	2014
The Élysée-Treaty is established as a treaty of friendship between West Germany and France.	Foundation of the Franco-German Office for Youth which follows the aim of creating an understanding and a close connection between France and Germany.	First payment of 'BAföG' for studying abroad (Federal Training Assistance Act for students at secondary schools and universities in Germany).	The Erasmus Program (European Region Action Scheme for the Mobility of University Students) is a European exchange programme for students.	Treaty on European Union (Maastricht Treaty)	Creation of the European Voluntary Service which enables young people aged 16–30 to volunteer in charitable institutions and broaden their experience.	The German volunteer programme 'Kulturweit', is established. It enables young people between 18 and 25 to participate for 6–12 months in a volunteer service.	Erasmus Plus is the newly organized European program for education and combines already existing programmes under one administration.	Creation of the U.S. Study Abroad Office

M1 Why Study Abroad?

Stacie Nevadomski Berdan

Stacie Nevadomski Berdan is an international consultant and author who focuses on global communication. Her cross-cultural experiences in different industries enabled her to write books on global education. In the following article, she presents her book *A Student Guide to Study Abroad*. Berdan is considered an expert on studying abroad programs and offers advice for the process of choosing a program, going abroad, immersing in the country and eventually returning to life in one's home country.

1. Think of pro and contra arguments for studying abroad and rank your ideas according to their importance.
2. **Present** Berdan's advice for students who want to study abroad.
3. **Compare** students' reasons for studying abroad with the expectations of a wide range of employers.
4. Create an advertising poster for a study abroad program in which you present the aims of the program and highlight the benefits. In doing so, develop ideas for a program which fulfil at least three of Berdan's recommendations for choosing the right program and be prepared to present it.

[...] So why do people study abroad? In research I conducted for my recently released book, *A Student Guide to Study Abroad*, students who had studied abroad in the past five years cited these top three reasons: experience another culture/country, travel and personal growth. Secondary reasons include career prospects and marketability*, learning a language and recommendations from a friend.

But when I followed up with employers across a vast spectrum of industries and sectors, asking them what they liked most about potential applicants who had studied abroad, they cited very practical applications of the experience:

- Creative problem solving experience in unfamiliar situations
- Adaptability* within culturally diverse environments
- Excellent listening and communication skills
- Practical knowledge of a specific culture and language

With the exception of language skills, these benefits fall into the all-important "soft skills" category growing in importance in the workplace. There is no doubt that studying abroad enhances* a student's resume, boosting her chances to impress a potential employer with her global outlook. But how do students – and their parents – decide which program is best? [...]

To help students get the most out of an experience abroad, programs should require intense language and academic preparation, research projects and presentations. Whether your program lasts three weeks or a full year, students should begin with significant cultural and intellectual preparation well before leaving campus, and conclude with an involved reentry and reintegration course.

For students interested in reaping* the rewards described above by employers, they'll need to choose a program that has a solid reputation for academic rigor and cross-cultural outreach. These programs should have entrance requirements and not just be open to anyone who can pay. Ideally they are integrated into your academic curriculum. Here are some specific program aspects to look for:

Local language coursework. Content classes (history, literature, business) taken in languages other than English demonstrate and improve language proficiency.

Diverse student bodies. Programs that attract participants from all over the world will be richer culturally. They also foster* greater proficiency in cross-cultural teamwork, thus better preparing students for similar work environments.

Regionally relevant content. Going abroad to study in a specific geographic and cultural context can enhance academic studies. Ideally, programs designed around a specific topic will include introductions to area experts and access to local information sources and perspectives.

Curricula-driven study abroad. Some programs bring global students together to work on a regional problem, such as water use rights, fair trade practices or cultural preservation. Working as a global team in an academic context is excellent preparation for global jobs.

Locations matters. Prospective* employers are increasingly interested in where applicants studied abroad. Branching out beyond the traditional European destinations and into countries such as China, Brazil, India, Mexico or Turkey, for example, signals an enhanced awareness of growing global economies – and a direct link to the places many organizations are expanding and growing.

In my talks on campuses, many students express an interest in "just having fun" while studying abroad, so they're planning on taking a few classes pass/fail and traveling around. They want to know, is that so wrong? It all depends on what the objective is. College is a time for fun and travel, yes, but it's primarily for becoming career-ready and developing skills that will lead to employment upon graduation. Study abroad offers students an opportunity to do both. [...]

Stacie Nevadomski Berdan, "Why study abroad", www.huffingtonpost.com, 10.10.2013 [23.09.2015]

marketability *here:* attractive CV for future employers

adaptability the ability to adjust to certain situations

to enhance to improve sth.

to reap to harvest sth.; to collect sth.

to foster to encourage sth.

prospective potential (adj.)

M2 Study Abroad Testimonials

StudyAbroad.com is an internet website which offers an overview over a vast variety of opportunities for going abroad. There is information to be found concerning different countries and various study programs as well as support for financing one's trip. Moreover, the following first-hand experiences of students are included to underline the importance of studying abroad.

1. **Point out** the different benefits of studying abroad as mentioned in the given testimonials.

2. In a silent writing exercise, develop word clusters for 'study abroad' in which you collect nouns/verbs/adjectives which are used when talking about studying abroad. You may use the testimonials as a start but can add more vocabulary whenever it comes to your mind. Possible aspects which can, for example, be put on different posters are: the individual learning process, language learning, culture, etc.

Gain a new perspective on life

"At first, I was extremely nervous about going abroad. I've always been a bit of a control-freak and I knew that while studying abroad in the Netherlands and traveling throughout Europe there would be so much out of my control. But, it was such an important opportunity for me to get out of my comfort zone. It put many things from my life in the States in perspective for me – relationships, careers, friendships. When I was abroad, I learned to go-with-the-flow more, which has truly made my post-abroad life easier. If you worry too much, you'll miss out on the amazing sights and experiences. I've taken that mentality back home with me and it truly is the best souvenir."
—Michelle King, studied abroad in the Netherlands

Become global-minded

"Studying abroad adds another level to your college experience. It takes you out of your element and places you in a place where you are less comfortable, enabling you to learn in a new way. Experiencing other cultures around the world broadens your knowledge base and teaches you to think and live differently. It is so important, today, to have a solid understanding of different cultures, and I think sending students abroad is an easy way to set up our generation to be a more globally-minded society."
—Emily O'Hara, studied abroad in England

Make unforgettable memories

"It's very easy to get homesick when you talk to your family and friends every day, but when I changed my routine, it became a lot easier to focus on my time spent in Europe than the time missed back home. Studying abroad is a great opportunity to get a crash course of the cities you always dream about, and the perfect chance to broaden your perspective in general."
—Shanae Burch, studied abroad in the Netherlands

Get out of your comfort zone

"Study abroad gave me the opportunity to explore that gray area of our lives called 'The Comfort Zone.' It brought me out of my nest at the College of Charleston and into a culture of new attitudes, values and beliefs. At times it was unbelievably frustrating, but the friends I made abroad helped me through the lows. And then they were there with me for

the highs! It was an extremely rewarding experience accentuated by the fact that, by the end of my stay, I had eaten frites and kebab for five months and was able to talk about American politics in French with the locals at the neighborhood laundromat*."
—Kyle Rees, studied abroad in Belgium

laundromat (AE) launderette (BE), place to wash one's clothes

Get to know yourself

"Studying abroad was an incredibly important semester for me. Being away for that long from your comfort zone forces you to analyze yourself, which can be really difficult but you come out a better person. I don't know anyone who wouldn't say the same; it's a huge opportunity for personal growth and development. For me personally, studying abroad in Paris allowed me to glimpse the kind of future I might want to lead. I'm a more independent and stronger person for the experience."
—Greg Nussen, studied abroad in France

Develop a new sense of independence

"Don't worry about missing out on what is going on here in the US. It's going to be happening for a long time, and you will be a part of it eventually. But for a semester, get out there and leave your comfort zone to experience a freedom and independence that will make you realize how much beauty there really is in this world. Then bring that experience back to all your friends at home and let them be so jealous!"
—Patrick McDonald, studied abroad in the Netherlands

Originally edited by: Valeri Boyle, "Study Abroad Testimonials", www.studyabroad.com, 25.07.2011 [25.09.2015]

Zoom in: Skills

Silent Writing Technique

In this activity, students communicate with each other by writing down their ideas. This technique has the aim of changing communication patterns in class. Students who do not display a lot of oral participation in class benefit in particular from this exercise since talking is not allowed.

Preparation:

- Group tables with posters have to be prepared.
- Each poster has the topic in its centre.
- Students are told the different topics of the posters.

Conducting the silent writing exercise:

- In their groups, the students start to write down all the words which come to their mind when considering the given topic.
- The students read the other students' ideas and can react to them by adding more words, for example from the same word family.
- The silent writing exercise ends after a given time, or when the students visibly run out of ideas.
- During this phase, no talking is allowed.

Evaluation:

- In a 'gallery walk', students can take a look at the results of other groups.
- Alternatively, students are asked to order the word cluster and to present it to the class afterwards. The class will then have to focus on language aspects and be prepared to correct mistakes.
- The posters should be made available to the students so that the clusters serve as an aid to learning vocabulary in class.

Adapted and taken from www.schulentwicklung.nrw.de [30.12.2015]

M3 My Life, My Hope – My Life as an Exchange Student

Anonymous

In the preface to the poem, the author does not give his/her name but describes his/her reasons for writing the poem as well as mentioning some details of his/her personal background. The person left his/her home country Ghana to study at a school in the US. Homesickness troubled the person and made it difficult to settle in, even though it had been his/her wish to participate in the intercultural program. However, with the support of friends and family, he/she found the courage to enjoy the stay abroad during the course of which the poem was written.

1. Pre-Reading: Choose three words from the word cloud which come to your mind when thinking about taking part in a school exchange.

2. While-Reading: **State** in one sentence what the individual stanzas deal with.

3. Post-Reading: On the basis of the poem, develop a flowchart and **outline** the feelings/expectations/difficulties of an exchange student.

4. **Analyse** the use of stylistic devices in the poem.

5. Imagine the different paragraphs to be e-mails written before and during the school exchange. From the perspective of a good friend, answer these e-mails.

I was scared, but I thought the experience was worth it
I was troubled and confused
I constantly shivered at the thought of leaving home
Of leaving all (the Beloveds) and places so (familiar to me)

To live in a land totally different and foreign from what I have been accustomed* to living
All because I never knew whether this land would be a foe* or a friend, welcoming or rejecting
And so for a moment, relying on blind fate as a safe refuge* I silently bore all my hopes.
Never had I ever thought of coming to this land as a teenager
For, all along, I only dreamed of seeing and experiencing her at the twilight of my life and not so early on, not having any clues as to what exactly to expect
... And yet, all this while, I was made aware I was coming to a great land; a land pregnant* with opportunities;
Which made me unceasingly wonder which kind of opportunities they were?
In my fickle-mindedness*, I feverishly* and fervently* went down on my knees,
Imploring* the best for the family I was yet to leave,
The school I was yet to miss,
And the friends I would soon be thinking of daily.
But amidst* all these concerns, I go ahead with my decision – my decision to leave
Even imploring the Family I so dearly love to let me go
With eyes soaked* in and with tears, they would have loved to say No
But telling them to have faith, hope and conviction that something good and worthwhile will surely come out of the adventure I was yet to make, I convince them to let me go.
[...]
The day finally came, with all its burdens* and difficult moments
The moment had come when I had to be gone for weeks and months and years
To be separated from my Family for as long a time as I could hardly imagine,
Pondering* just how my friends would not even be able to shed the tears so hidden, for fear of making parting* more difficult than it was for us
At that point, I decided against my decision,
I decided I was only crazy to think of leaving;
[...]
Amidst all the confusion and tears, I trudged* on until I finally found myself in a completely different milieu,
Welcomed and embraced* by folks I knew too little about, and beset* with strange challenges, I fought the urge* to give in to doubt and fear, strived* to keep to my vows, my dreams and my aspirations
I know I am now in an environment that requires me to love, to tolerate new and diverse people all over again, and to work harder
I never envisaged* it would be as difficult and strenuous as it presently is
[...]
Anyway
I met a loving family whom I instantly loved upon meeting them; who constantly encouraged me and made me know that they cared
Though things are different and difficult and interesting,
I always reminded myself that
'That was how things were with me and nothing was going to change that'
[...]
As determined as I am, the only message I can depart* with now is
Expect more from me and the difference I bring into your lives.

Anonymous, "My Life, My Hope – My Life as an Exchange Student", www.teenink.com [15.09.2015]

to be accustomed to to be used to
foe enemy
refuge shelter, asylum
pregnant *schwanger*
fickle-minded *wankelmütig*
feverishly *fieberhaft*
fervently *leidenschaftlich*
to implore to beg
amidst in the middle of
soaked drenched, covered in
burden stress
to ponder to consider
to part to leave, to move away from each other
to trudge to walk slowly with heavy steps
embraced *umarmt*
to beset *bedrängen*
urge need
to strive to try very hard to achieve sth.
to envisage [ɪnˈvɪzːɪdʒ] to imagine
to depart to leave, *here:* to give a message

M 4 Deciding to Study Abroad Can Be Tricky for Minority Ethnic Students

Fedora Abu

Fedora Abu is a student of French and Italian at University College in London. She is the founder and editor-in-chief of the magazine *Citoyenne*, an online magazine for young London women. The following article was published in the online students section of *The Guardian*.

1. **Point out** possible problems which ethnic minority students may encounter while studying abroad.

2. **Examine** the author's line of argumentation.

3. Imagine you are Falcone's (foreign student in Luxembourg) best friend in England. After she told you that "[it] made [her] more wary of becoming friends with people because of the inevitable comments they would make" (ll. 35 f.), write a letter to her in which you **comment** on the article and offer advice.

build-up time of preparation
bureaucracy [bju'rɒkrəsi] *Bürokratie*
concern worry
to head to to move into a certain direction

[...] Preparing to study abroad is nerve-wracking whoever you are. It may be exciting, but the build-up* can also be stressful: from finding a place to live to navigating foreign bureaucracy*.
However, for many minority ethnic students, there can often be an added concern*, particularly when heading* to countries that are less racially diverse or tolerant than the UK. Speaking to BME (black and minority ethnic) students who've studied abroad, it seems the extent to which they experienced racism largely depended on where they chose to study.
Anita Barton-Williams, a Nottingham Trent University graduate, spent her year abroad in Strasbourg, France, and at the University of Salamanca's Avila campus in Spain. Her experiences – and those of her friends – led her to write an article advising other BME students.
"I did some research before I chose where to go, but definitely not enough. I wish I'd found out which political parties were in power," admits Barton-Williams, who arrived in Strasbourg to find it was Front National* territory.
Finding accommodation also proved a problem, with one estate agent* saying they weren't having much progress because they were black. "I got lucky and found a place with a Guadeloupean*, but two of my black guy friends really struggled. Eventually, they ended up living with a Martiniquais* lady who rented to them out of empathy."
In Spain, Barton-Williams hoped that being in a small town such as Avila would help with her Spanish, but soon found that being black made her and her friends local celebrities – people would stare and cross the road "to get a closer look".
Fortunately, they were welcomed by the town's small Dominican community, but Barton-Williams thinks having other BME students with her was what helped her cope*. "If I hadn't gone with my group of friends, I would've probably quit my year abroad because there was no support."
Selena Falcone decided to study her whole psychology degree at the University of Luxembourg instead of the UK, with a term at Sophia University in Japan, and quickly noticed the difference in attitudes to race compared to the UK.

Front National French nationalist political party with a right-wing program, known for its opposition to immigration
estate agent a person who is selling houses
Guadeloupean [gwɑːdə'luːpiːən] a person who is from Guadeloupe island (part of the French Antilles)
Martiniquais [maːtɪ'niːkeɪ] a person from the island of Martinique
to cope with to deal with

"It's something people are more aware of in Luxembourg and Japan. In Luxembourg, what shocked me were the casual comments people would make about black people as if they didn't concern me, because my appearance can be misleading," says Falcone, who is of Eritrean, German and Italian descent*.

"My background suddenly became relevant, whereas in England I never had to think about it. It made me more wary* of becoming friends with people because of the inevitable comments they would make."

By contrast, picking a diverse place in which to study can leave you feeling a lot more welcome. Cecilia Effa, a student at the University of Birmingham, spent a year of her English and Creative Writing degree at New Mexico State University in the US, staying in Las Cruces.

"Las Cruces was a fantastic place with a huge mix of cultures", says Effa, who is of Iranian and Nigerian heritage. "There were a ton of Hispanic, black and mixed race people, and a huge Native American and Mexican influence as well. There really wasn't much potential for racism – I never had anyone say anything negative about my race." [...]

Universities should put minority ethnic students in touch with BME students and alumni who've studied abroad so they can hear their experiences. [...]

That being said, responsibility also lies with students themselves, who know whether or not they're willing to sacrifice visiting a diverse place to experience a particular* culture, country or city.

And while it's not fair that minority ethnic students may feel they have to limit their choices because of their race, it's important they take such factors into account so they can get the most out of their experience studying abroad.

Fedora Abu, "Deciding to Study Abroad Can Be Tricky For Minority Ethnic Students", www.theguardian.co.uk, 22.08.2015 [24.09.2015]

descent a person's family origins

wary ['weəri] careful

particular specific

M 5 Remarks by the First Lady at the Standford Center at Peking University

Michelle Obama

On a trip to China in 2014, Michelle Obama spoke at the Stanford Center at Peking University to an audience of American students studying in China and Chinese students who had studied in the USA. In a press release, the White House underlined that the weeklong trip intended to highlight the importance of global education and foreign exchange programs.

ZOOM IN: People

Michelle La Vaughn Robinson Obama is an African-American lawyer and writer in the United States and First Lady to the 44th president of the USA, Barack Obama.
She was born on 17 January 1964 in Chicago, Illinois, to Fraser Robinson, a pump operator at the Chicago Water Department, and Marian Robinson. Michelle Obama attended public schools in Chicago's South Side and followed her brother to Princeton University, where she pursued a Bachelor of Arts in Sociology and African American Studies. She graduated from Harvard Law School in 1988 and started to work as a lawyer for a Chicago law firm. She met her future husband, Barack Obama, when they were co-working as lawyers in Chicago. The couple were married in 1992 and they have two daughters, Malia Ann (*1998) and Natasha (*2001).
Michelle Obama worked as Associate Dean of Student Services at the University of Chicago where she focused on developing the Community Service Center, which led to an increase in volunteerism.
Obama supported her husband's campaign for the presidential election. Barack Obama was inaugurated as president on 20 January 2009, his wife Michelle becoming First Lady at the White House. Obama was re-elected president in November 2012. In both terms, Michelle Obama used her position to promote programmes for poverty awareness, children's nutrition and physical activity. She launched programmes such as 'Let's Move' (against child obesity), Joining Forces (support for military members as well as their families), Reach Higher (supporting young people in achieving higher education) and 'Let Girls Learn' (initiative to enable girls worldwide to go to school).

1. Obama delivered this speech in Beijing with the aim of promoting global education. She gives a number of reasons for studying abroad. Which reasons do you expect the U.S. government to stress when promoting study abroad programmes?

@ SNG-40660-001

Listening

2. **Compare** Obama's reasons for study abroad programs with the reasons given in the student testimonials (p. 10/11) and **explain** possible differences and similarities.

3. Do further research on the U.S. study abroad program which is run by the Bureau of Educational and Cultural Affairs (www.studyabroad.state.gov). Imagine you are a member of a student council at a U.S. High School and have to prepare a 5-minute talk on the study abroad programme and its benefits for American high school students. Consider stories relating to personal experiences and financial aspects as well as travel information.

M 6 Americanah: Studying Abroad in the United States

Chimamanda Ngozi Adichie

Chimamanda Ngozi Adichie is a Nigerian author whose novel *Americanah* was published in 2013 and since then has won various international awards. The novel deals with two young Nigerians, Ifemelu and Obinze, in love with each other but ready to separate and leave the country during the time of military dictatorship. In the following excerpt, Ifemelu has recently taken up her studies at university in Philadelphia and describes her first encounter with fellow African students.

Zoom in: People

Chimamanda Ngozi Adichie is a well-known Nigerian author who has won numerous literary awards for her novels and short stories, among them the Orange Prize. Her work has been translated into thirty languages.
Born in 1977 to a university professor and a university administrator, Adichie grew up in Nsukka, Nigeria. After successfully completing secondary education at the university's school, she started to study at the University of Nigeria. One and a half years later, she gained a scholarship to study in Philadelphia, USA,
where she graduated summa cum laude in 2001 with a degree in Communication and Political Science. Following this, she pursued a degree in Creative Writing at John Hopkins University, Baltimore. On top of this, she went on to gain a Master's degree in African studies from Yale University in 2008.
While still at university, she started working on her first novel. After this first literary success, she continued to write and was awarded a fellowship by the Radcliffe Institute for Advanced Study at Harvard University which allowed her to finish her third novel *Americanah*, published in 2013.
She lives in Nigeria as well as in the United States.

1. **Outline** the cultural differences which African students have to face when arriving in the US according to Mwombeki.
2. **Analyse** how humour is created in Mwombeki's welcome speech.
3. **Examine** the presentation of American daily life in the following excerpt.
4. **Discuss** whether or not Mwombeki's advice that it is important to find friends among fellow international students is helpful when it comes to fulfilling the aims of studying abroad.
5. **Contrast** the perspective of African students in the USA with the presentation of minority students in M 4.

[...] Wambui had told everyone that Ifemelu was looking for a job. Dorothy, the girly Ugandan with long braids who worked as a waitress in Center City, said her restaurant was hiring. But first, Mwombeki, the Tanzanian double major in engineering and political science, looked over Ifemelu's résumé* and asked her to delete the three years of univer-

résumé ['rəzumeɪ] (AE) curriculum vitae [kəˌrɪkjuləm 'viːteɪ], CV (BE) sity in Nigeria: American employers did not like lower-level employees to be too educated. Mwombeki reminded her of Obinze, that ease about him, that quiet strength. At meetings, he made everyone laugh. "I got a good primary education because of Nyerere's socialism," Mwombeki said often. "Otherwise I would be in Dar* right now, carving* ugly giraffes for tourists." When two new students came for the first time, one from Ghana and the other from Nigeria, Mwombeki gave them what he called the welcome talk.

"Please do not go to Kmart* and buy twenty pairs of jeans because each costs five dollars. The jeans are not running away. They will be there tomorrow at an even more reduced price. You are now in America: do not expect to have hot food for lunch. That African taste must be abolished*. When you visit the home of an American with some money, they will offer to show you their house. Forget that in your house back home, your father would have thrown a fit* if anyone came close to his bedroom. We all know that the living room was where it stopped and, if absolutely necessary, then the toilet. But please smile and follow the American and see the house and make sure you say you like everything. And do not be shocked by the indiscriminate* touching of American couples. Standing in line at the cafeteria, the girl will touch the boy's arm and the boy will put his arm around her shoulder and they will rub shoulders and back and rub rub rub, but please do not imitate this behaviour."

They were all laughing. Wambui shouted something in Swahili*.

"Very soon you will start to adopt an American accent, because you don't want customer service people on the phone to keep asking you 'What? What?' You will start to admire Africans who have perfect American accents, like our brother here, Kofi. Kofi's parents came from Ghana when he was two years old, but do not be fooled by the way he sounds. If you go to their house, they eat kenkey* every day. His father slapped him when he got a C in a class. There's no American nonsense in that house. He goes back to Ghana every year. We call people like Kofi American-Africans, not African-American, which is what we call out brothers and sisters whose ancestors were slaves."

"It was a B minus, not a C," Kofi quipped.

"Try and make friends with our African-American brothers and sisters in a spirit of true pan-Africanism. But make sure you remain friends with fellow Africans, as this will help you keep your perspective. Always attend African Students Association meetings, but if you must, you can also try the Black Student Union. Please note that in general, African Americans go to the Black Student Union and Africans go to the African Students Association. Sometimes it overlaps but not a lot. The Africans who go to BSU are those with no confidence who are quick to tell you 'I am *originally* from Kenya' even though Kenya pops out the minute they open their mouths. The African Americans who come to our meetings are the ones who write poems about Mother Africa and think every African is a Nubian* queen. If an African American calls you a Mandingo or a booty scratcher, he is insulting you for being African. Some will ask you annoying questions about Africa, but others will connect with you. You will also find that you might make friends more easily with other internationals, Koreans, Indians, Brazilians, whatever, than with Americans both black and white. Many of the internationals understand the trauma of trying to get an American visa and that is a good place to start a friendship."

There was more laughter, Mwombeki himself laughing loudly, as though he had not heard his own jokes before. [...]

Chimamanda Ngozi Adichie, *Americanah*, Anchor Books, New York 2013, p. 171–173

Dar es Salaam [ˌdɑːressəˈlɑːm] capital city of Tanzania
to carve to cut wood into artful sculptures
Kmart US retailer which offers everything from clothing, furniture and grocery to jewellery
to abolish sth. to get rid of sth.
to throw a fit to be angry about sth.

indiscriminate thoughtless

Swahili [swɑːˈhiːli] language spoken in East Africa, especially among people who speak different first languages
kenkey (traditional food mainly from Ghana) maize is cooked and prepared as a side dish for meat or fish

Nubia former kingdom in northern Africa and one of the earliest civilizations
Nubian queen in modern language, the term refers to a woman with African heritage

6. In her speech 'The Danger of a Single Story' delivered at a TedX event and published on YouTube (see Webcode), Adichie explains how a story, told from a single perspective, has the power to become the only story to be told. Practise looking at different perspectives of a story by writing your own 'single story'. For that, decide on a news item from a country which is not often in the news and do research on aspects of that country. In groups, present your 'single stories' to each other and together decide on an appropriate presentation of these diverse stories.

@ SNG-40660-002

M 7 Found in Pieces

Ian Lancaster

Ian Lancaster was a student at the University of Colorado Boulder and took part in a study abroad programme which took him to Florence, Italy. Inspired by this experience, he wrote down his thoughts in this poem.

1. Have a look at the photograph and based on this, make an educated guess about what the poem 'Found in Pieces' may deal with.
2. **Examine** the use of imagery in the poem.
3. **Explain** the narrator's statement that he "found pieces of [himself] all over the world" (l. 15).
4. **Evaluate** whether the title 'Found in Pieces' may serve as an appropriate heading for all kinds of intercultural experiences.

I could never tell you where I'm going, but I can always tell you where I've been.
Yet reciting* the places I traveled and the things I tasted seem like blasphemy or sin.
I've taken my life and packed it into a bag once, twice, three, ok more than a few more times.

to recite to repeat or utter aloud

But I did so without much care, much like a person who's reading a book who can't see between the lines.
I moved from state to state, and now I move from country to country.
I think about the mountains I've crossed with towers and clouds below me.
The air of *The Top of Europe* has grazed* my face while I've bombed* down the mountain.
But it was the atmosphere of Spain – hot in intrigue, history, and beauty – that poured like an endless fountain.
Now every moment as I grab my bag to go.
I never think of rain, sunshine, or snow.
I've found pieces of myself all over the world.
So I think ...
How many hidden pieces of me does this world hold?
Every time I arrive at a new destination I discover pieces of myself.
I see some of me in the dates of SW Asia, streets of Seville, and also the cafes in France.
I've been enamored* with conversation with a bella donna that left me in a trance.
A constant intrigue of self and world exploration.
A perfect movie with only nature's narration.
I may now be sitting atop a mountain, a shore of the beach, or on a small boat in the middle of the ocean
But wherever I am, I remember I'm not living unless my life is in **motion**.

Ian Lancaster, "Found in Pieces", http://capaworld.capa.org, 28.06.2013 [24.09.2015]

to graze to brush sth. lightly
to bomb down to move very fast

enamored (AE) [ɪ'næmərd], enamoured (BE) [ɪ'næməd] *here*: charmed, captivated

M 8a Deutschland ist weltoffen

Deutscher Akademischer Austauschdienst (DAAD)

Wissenschaft weltoffen is a German publication which focuses on the conditions of studying and doing research in Germany. The Federal Ministry of Education and Research annually publishes the magazine in which the German Academic Exchange Service (DAAD) analyses Germany's role in global research and knowledge.

1. Imagine you are a foreign student visiting a German university and have come across the following press release by the Ministry of Education. In your blog about your stay in Germany you **present** the content of the following press release to your fellow students at your home university.

Noch nie waren an deutschen Hochschulen mehr ausländische Studierende eingeschrieben* als heute. Auch nach dem Studienabschluss bleibt jeder zweite ausländische Absolvent* zunächst in Deutschland – deutlich mehr als bisher angenommen. Fast alle ausländischen Absolventen sind gut in den Arbeitsmarkt integriert. Gleichzeitig gehen deutsche Studentinnen und Studenten im internationalen Vergleich besonders häufig für studien-

einschreiben to enrol
Absolvent graduate

bezogene Aufenthalte ins Ausland. Das geht aus dem Bericht „Wissenschaft weltoffen 2014“ hervor, den das Bundesministerium für Bildung und Forschung* (BMBF) gemeinsam mit dem Deutschen Akademischen Austauschdient* (DAAD) und dem Deutschen Zentrum für Hochschul- und Wissenschaftsforschung (DZHW) vorgestellt hat.

„Deutschland ist bei ausländischen Studierenden so beliebt wie nie zuvor. Deutsche Hochschulen sind internationale Orte geworden“, sagte Bildungsministerin* Johanna Wanka. „Für Forschung oder Studium eine Zeit im Ausland zu verbringen und an den Hochschulen mit ausländischen Kommilitonen* und Lehrenden zusammen zu arbeiten, ist heute eine Selbstverständlichkeit. Exzellente Wissenschaft braucht den internationalen Austausch. Grundvoraussetzung dafür sind weltoffene Hochschulen, an denen vom Professor über das Verwaltungspersonal bis hin zu den Studierenden eine Willkommenskultur gelebt wird.“

„Die internationale Attraktivität eines Hochschul- und Forschungsstandorts* misst sich daran, wie viele ausländische Studierende von einem Land angezogen werden. Die Tatsache, dass auch so viele von ihnen bleiben, zeigt, dass Deutschland für Talente aus aller Welt ein Anziehungspunkt ist“, sagte DAAD-Präsidentin Margret Wintermantel.

Deutschland ist nach den USA und Großbritannien für ausländische Studierende das beliebteste Gastland. Die Zahl aller ausländischen Studierenden lag im Wintersemester 2013/14 erstmals über der Marke von 300 000, damit kommt etwa jeder zehnte Student in Deutschland aus dem Ausland. Besonders groß ist der Zustrom in Masterstudiengänge. Überproportional* viele Ausländer studieren in Deutschland Ingenieursdisziplinen*. Der Ausländeranteil an den Hochschulangehörigen liegt bei etwa 10 Prozent – rund 35 300 wissenschaftliche und künstlerische Mitarbeiter mit ausländischer Staatsbürgerschaft waren 2012 an deutschen Hochschulen beschäftigt.

Rund 134 000 Deutsche studierten im Jahr 2011 im Ausland, etwa jeder dritte Studierende in Deutschland absolvierte während seines Studiums einen studienbezogenen Auslandsaufenthalt. Die deutschen Studierenden sind im Vergleich zu den meisten anderen Ländern überdurchschnittlich mobil, auch wenn die Mobilitätsquoten seit dem Jahr 2000 weitgehend unverändert sind. Die Bundesregierung und der DAAD haben sich das Ziel gesetzt, dass bis 2020 jeder zweite deutsche Hochschulabsolvent Auslandserfahrung gesammelt haben soll.

Ein Schwerpunkt von „Wissenschaft weltoffen“ widmet sich in diesem Jahr den akademischen Austauschbeziehungen zwischen USA und Deutschland. Nach Kanada und Großbritannien ist Deutschland für US-amerikanische Studierende, die im Ausland eingeschrieben sind, das wichtigste Gastland. Bei den deutschen Studierenden ist hingegen im letzten Jahrzehnt ein rückläufiges Interesse gegenüber den USA als Studienziel festzustellen. Bei Naturwissenschaftlern* aus den USA ist Deutschland inzwischen wichtigstes nicht-englischsprachiges Gastland.

Investitionen der Bundesregierung etwa in den Hochschulpakt* oder den Pakt für Forschung und Innovation unterstützen die Internationalisierung der Wissenschaft ebenso wie die Förderung der spezifischen Programme von Organisationen wie dem DAAD oder der Alexander von Humboldt-Stiftung. Im Haushalt 2014 wurden die Mittel für Studenten- und Wissenschaftleraustausch sowie internationale Hochschul- und Wissenschaftskooperation um zehn Millionen Euro auf 140,5 Millionen Euro angehoben und sollen auch in den kommenden Jahren auf diesem Niveau fortgeschrieben werden.

„Wissenschaft Weltoffen“ ist das Referenzwerk zur internationalen Mobilität von Studierenden und Wissenschaftlern. Der DAAD analysiert darin die Rolle Deutschlands im weltweiten Wissensaustausch. Der Bericht entsteht in Kooperation mit dem DZHW und wird finanziert vom BMBF und dem Auswärtigen Amt.

Christina Brüning, Simone Burkhart, Ulrich Heublein, „Deutschland ist weltoffen“, www.bmbf.de, 15.07.2014 [24.09.2015]

Bundesministerium für Bildung und Forschung Federal Ministry of Education and Research
Deutscher Akademischer Austauschdienst German Academic Exchange Service
Bildungsministerin Minister of Education
Kommilitone fellow student

Hochschul- und Forschungsstandort academic and research site/location

überproportional disproportional
Ingenieursdisziplin engineering discipline

Naturwissenschaftler scientist

Hochschulpakt pact of institutions of tertiary education

M 8b Deutsche und ausländische Studienanfänger ab 1995

1. Analyse the statistical data. What does it suggest about Germany as an open and tolerant country?

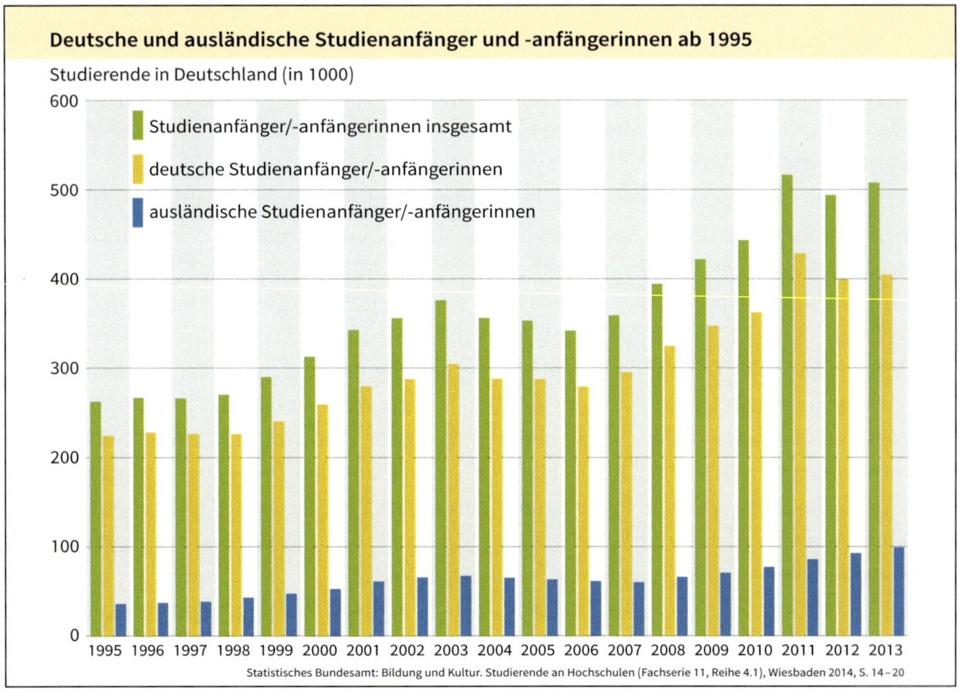

Statistisches Bundesamt: Bildung und Kultur. Studierende an Hochschulen (Fachserie 11, Reihe 4.1), Wiesbaden [erschienen am 03.09.2014], S. 14–20.

Zoom in: Vocabulary

Talking about statistics

- The bar chart shows/depicts/illustrates/is about/provides information about ...
- The figures refer to ...
- With the help of the bar chart, we can see how ...
- Between 1995 and 2013 ...
- From 1995 to 2013 ...

Increases

- ... a strong upward trend
- ... a slight/steady/constant/substantial increase in ...
- ... an overall increase can be seen in ...
- ... numbers have continued to rise since ...

Decreases

- ... a slight/notable/significant decrease in ...
- ... numbers have continued to fall

Fluctuations

- ... occasional fluctuations/a slight drop in/occasional variations due to ...
- ... an initial upward trend was followed by ...

M 9 10 Things to Know Before Studying in Germany

Caitlin Hardee

Born in Seattle, USA, Caitlin Hardee is freelance writer, who is currently living in the city of her choice, Berlin. She studied German Philology and spent a year as a foreign student in Berlin. After finishing her studies, she was awarded a journalist scholarship of the German Academic Exchange Service (DAAD) and returned to Germany. Since then, she has been writing on various topics and is the editor of the blog *Nomad News* which deals with grass-roots culture and news journalism.

"So we agree: having attained diversity, we must now categorise, coordinate, and consolidate it."

1. Describe the cartoon and take an educated guess about what the article may deal with.
2. Write down 10 pieces of advice which you would give to foreign students before they go to Germany.
3. **Present** the image of Germany which is given in the article.
4. **Examine** the tone of the text.
5. **Evaluate** the way Germany is presented in the text by arguing for or against it.

to outsource *ausgliedern*

enticing tempting, appealing

nexus *Verknüpfung*

to salivate *here:* to have a lot of saliva in your mouth because you see something you want

revelry celebration

flawless faultless, without mistake

to tip the scales to decide matters

infringement violation

perks benefits, bonuses

savvy clever

intrepid [in'trepid] fearless

In the United States, the average student loan debt is nearing $30,000. In the UK, it's closer to $66,000. For millennials, outsourcing* higher education is becoming increasingly attractive.

One enticing* destination is Germany. The land of poets and thinkers is famed for its practically nonexistent tuition fees at public universities, along with its high quality of life and a location at the nexus* of European culture and politics. But while students with wanderlust in their blood might salivate* over visions of free college paired with beer-soaked revelry* at the Oktoberfest [...], there are some practical things you should know before jumping on a plane to Germany. [...]

4. The immigrant struggle is real

Unless you are an EU citizen, expect to spend a decent amount of time dealing with the *Ausländerbehörde* (foreigners' office). [...]

Still, be prepared for unexpected snags and understand that your starry-eyed dreams are of no interest to anybody within German bureaucracy. You are responsible for getting your act together and navigating the various hurdles of obtaining health insurance, demonstrating financial independence, finding an apartment, registering yourself at the *Bürgeramt* (local administrative office), scheduling a visa appointment, and having all your documents organized. [...]

5. Become a paperwork ninja

On that note, you'll need to embrace paperwork in general. Familiarize yourself with the conventions of German business letters and bureaucratic language. Keep copies of everything. Be flawlessly* organized and quick on the draw with documents. This will tip the scales* in your favor in situations ranging from visa battles to snatching a sweet apartment out from under the nose of some yuppie couple with regular jobs, to demanding rent reductions for infringements* of your renters' rights. [...]

7. German universities will not hold your hand

Here's the thing about the American private college experience: After laying down $50,000 or so per year, you get all kinds of "free" perks* thrown in, from laundry facilities to live entertainment and on-campus health clinics. [...]

Not so in Germany. It's on you to figure everything out, survive in a strange country, attend lectures, and study. You only get out what you put in! Also, while certain seminars more closely resemble an interactive liberal arts model and factor in participation and homework, a fair number of courses pin the entire grade on the final exam or paper.

8. Student housing is a snoozefest

Some large German universities do have official student housing, after a fashion – whether a small *Studentendorf* or urban blocks of designated student-only apartment buildings with spartan singles. Chances are, these options are neither the most attractive flats nor your best chance of acquiring a stellar social life.

Instead, brush up on your charm and apply to join a lively flatshare, known throughout Germany as a WG, or *Wohngemeinschaft*. Living in a larger WG with a number of Germans is a fantastic strategy for meeting locals and expanding your friend circle in a hurry – not to mention your language skills. [...]

10. Fair warning: You may want to stay forever

Free education? Excellent. You are a savvy*, intrepid* individual who knows how to get the best out of life. You'll just chill out in *Deutschland* for a few years, snag that degree, maybe work for a bit, and then come home to make the big bucks, right? Maybe. Or you might fall irrevocably in love with Germany. [...]

Caitlin Hardee, "10 Things to Know Before Studying In Germany", www.dw.com, 23.01.2015 [08.09.2015]

Gap Year – the Good, the Bad and the Ugly

M 1 Itchy Feet

Horrorshow

Horrorshow is an Australian hip hop duo that has been active since 2006. On their Facebook page they introduce themselves as Adit who "makes all the beats" and Solo who "talks all the shit".

1. "To have/get itchy feet" is an idiomatic expression that puts the wish to travel or move to a different place or to want to do something different into words. In a Think! Pair! Share! activity reflect on whether you have itchy feet or not and explain your reasons.

Listening

2. **Describe** the situation the protagonist finds himself in.
3. **Examine** in how far the choice of words illustrates the protagonist's urge to travel.
4. Listen to the song again and concentrate on the combination of instruments and vocals. **Explain** how the type of music, the beat and the singing style reflect the song's message. Make use of the language support provided.
5. Imagine you are the protagonist of the song. Write a letter to a friend or a relative in which you **discuss** the reasons for and the outcome of your travels.

He woke up, didn't really know how he got there
Wasn't too sure why neither
A believer of sorts
Just not too sure what sort of belief to believe in
So when the sun goes down each evening
He looks to the sky for a reason
Wonders what's behind the horizon
So he packs light and he's off and he's leaving
So he walks on looking for something
But just what it is, well he wasn't too sure
So he walked all day, then he walked all night
Then he walked all year, then he walked some more
Then he ... then he stopped
Took a look around to just see where he'd got to
Didn't recognise the spot so he took it all in
Got his things, and he up and moved on

Adit (left) and Solo (right) from *Horrorshow*

[Chorus: (2x)]
We roam* all over the planet looking for answers
Cross over timezones, connect the dots on the atlas
So as this world keeps turning around on its axis
On we march with itchy feet, there's always somewhere you could be

to roam to move about or travel, especially without a clear idea of where you are going

to swap to exchange

to intersect to cross one another

dead of night the middle of the night

scenic (adj.) having or allowing you to see beautiful natural features

So he walked all over the land
Over snow and desert sands
Through valleys and mountains, cities and towns
When he got to the ocean he swam
When it was too far, he learnt to fly
Built a set of wings and he took to the sky
So he looked high and low
Tryn'a find what it's like on the other side
And everywhere that he went he'd ask people questions
Swapped* stories and traded perspectives
Each moving in different directions
Paths on the map just intersecting*
And though the names and the faces changed
Some things remained the same
And some spoke with words he couldn't understand
But some things you don't need words to say
And then one day, he looks back and sees how far he's come
All the faces he's met on the way since he left
From the place that he started from
All living off the food that they learnt how to grow
And the rules that they learnt to know
So he took everything that he'd learnt from them
And he set off to look for home

[Repeat Chorus: (2x)]

[Repeat (3x)]
Left, right, left, right
Catch me on the next flight
Onward through the dead of night*
Searching for a fresh sky
Over land, over sea
Planet never goes to sleep
On we march with itchy feet
There's always somewhere you could be, say

He woke up, still didn't know how he got there
Still wasn't sure why either
A believer of sorts
Believes in the faith that he found in the places he's been in
When the sun goes down each evening
He's dreaming of somewhere scenic*
Behind the horizon there's a whole world to see
He won't stop till he's seen it

Zoom in: Vocabulary

Talking about the song

The music is ...

- instrumental – rhythmic – powerful – catchy – optimistic – dissonant – melodious – soft – loud – lively – energetic – fast – slow – sad – uplifting – cheerful – monotonous – ...

The music ...

- creates a feeling of suspense – threat – happiness – joy – sadness – ...

The song has ...

- a pleasant – catchy – ... melody
- a simple rhythm – chorus – ...

The mood is ...

- sad – aggressive – calming – angry – excited – relaxing – moving – joyful – optimistic – disturbing – harsh – bitter – ...

The singer's voice is ...

- deep – husky – hoarse – high-pitched – soothing – ...

M 2 Neither Here Nor There. Travels in Europe

Bill Bryson

Neither Here Nor There is best-selling author Bill Bryson's fourth book on travelling. This humorous travelogue was published in 1991 and documents Bryson's tour of Europe one year before and also refers to his early trips in the summers of 1972 and 1973. In the following extract the American describes his view of Europe, the Europeans, and the wonders of travelling in general.

To my mind, the greatest reward and luxury of travel is to be able to experience everyday things as if for the first time, to be in a position in which almost nothing is so familiar it is taken for granted.
Bill Bryson

1. Have a look at Bryson's introduction to *The Best American Travel Writing* 2000 that is given in the speech bubble on p. 27. What does it reveal about the author's view on travelling? Do you agree? Talk to a partner.

2. **Outline** what struck the author when visiting Europe.

3. **Explain** what Bryson means when he states that "you could never be sure of anything in Europe" (l. 56 f.) and **examine** the way he uses stereotypes to reinforce that statement.

4. Against the backdrop of your own experiences growing up in Europe, **evaluate** the author's observations.

5. **Discuss** whether Bryson's first impressions would be different today given that the world has changed a lot since 1972. In how far would they differ?

The first time I came to Europe was in 1972, skinny, shy, alone. In those days the only cheap flights were from New York to Luxembourg, with a refuelling stop en route at Keflavik Airport at Reykjavik. [...]

I had brought with me a yellow backpack so enormous that when I went through customs I half expected to be asked, 'Anything to declare? Cigarettes? Alcohol? Dead horse?', and spent the day teetering* beneath it through ancient streets of Luxembourg City in a kind of vivid daze* – an unfamiliar mixture of excitement and exhaustion and intense optical stimulation. Everything seemed so vivid and acutely focused and new. I felt like someone stepping out of doors for the first time. It was all so different: the language, the money, the cars, the number plates on the cars, the bread, the food, the newspapers, the parks, the people. I had never seen a zebra-crossing before, never seen a tram, never seen an unsliced loaf of bread (never even considered it an option), never seen anyone wearing a beret* who expected to be taken seriously, never seen people go to a different shop for each item of dinner or provide their own shopping bags, never seen feathered pheasants* and unskinned rabbits hanging in a butcher's window or a pig's head smiling on a platter, never seen a packet of Gitanes* or the Michelin man*. And the people – why, they were Luxemburgers. I don't know why this amazed me so, but it did. I kept thinking, that man over there, he's a Luxemburger. And so is that girl. They don't know anything about the New York Yankees, they don't know the theme tune to the Mickey Mouse Club, they are from another world. It was just wonderful. [...]

Sometimes a nation's little contrivances* are so singular and clever that we associate them with that country alone – double-decker buses in Britain, windmills in Holland (what an inspired addition to a flat landscape: think how they could transform Nebraska), sidewalk cafés in Paris. And yet there are some things that most countries do without difficulty that others cannot get a grasp of at all.

The French, for instance, cannot get the hang of queuing*. They try and try, but it is beyond them. Wherever you go in Paris, you see orderly lines waiting at a bus stop, but as soon as the bus pulls up, the line instantly disintegrates into something like a fire drill at lunatic asylum* as everyone scrambles* to be the first aboard, quite unaware that this defeats the whole object of queuing. The British, on the other hand, do not understand certain of the fundamentals of eating, as evidenced by their instinct to consume hamburgers with a knife and fork. To my continuing amazement, many of them also turn their fork upside-down and balance food on the back of it. I've lived in England for a decade and a half and I still have to quell* an impulse to go up to strangers in pubs and restaurants and say, 'Excuse me, can I give you a tip that'll help stop those peas bouncing all over the table?'.

to teeter to move in an unsteady way
daze confused state
beret a round flat cap
pheasant *Fasan*
Gitanes a French brand of cigarettes
Michelin man symbol of the tyre company Michelin
contrivance *here*: invention, device, contraption
to queue to line up
lunatic asylum psychiatric hospital
to scramble to move hastily
to quell to suppress

Germans are flummoxed* by humour, the Swiss have no concept of fun, the Spanish think there is nothing at all ridiculous about eating dinner at midnight, and the Italians should never, ever have been let in on the innovation of the motor car.

flummoxed confused

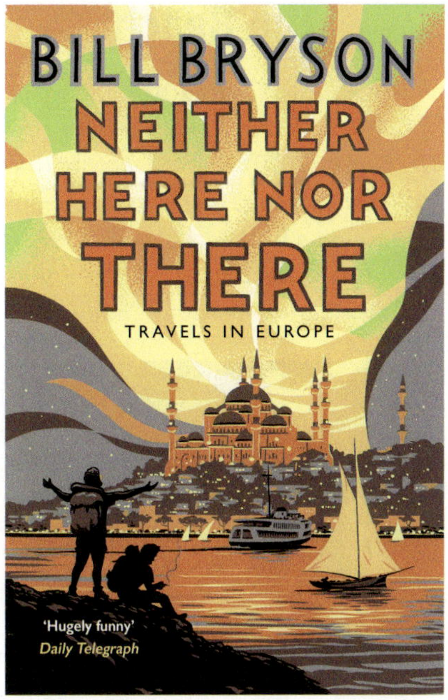

One of the small marvels of my first trip to Europe was the discovery that the world could be so full of variety, that there were so many different ways of doing essentially identical things, like eating and drinking and buying cinema tickets. It fascinated me that Europeans could at once be so alike – that they could be so universally bookish and cerebral*, and drive small cars, and live in little houses in ancient towns, and love soccer, and be relatively unmaterialistic and law-abiding*, and have chilly hotel rooms and cosy and inviting places to eat and drink – and yet be so endlessly, unpredictably different from each other as well. I loved the idea that you could never be sure of anything in Europe. [...]

cerebral relating to the brain

law-abiding obeying the law

When I told friends in London that I was going to travel around Europe and write a book about it, they said, 'Oh, you must speak a lot of languages.' 'Why, no,' I would reply with a certain pride, 'only English,' and they would look at me as if I were crazy. But that's the glory of foreign travel, as far as I'm concerned. I don't want to know what people are talking about. I can't think of anything that excites a greater sense of childlike wonder than to be in a country where you are ignorant of almost everything. Suddenly you're five years old again. You can't read anything, you have only the most rudimentary sense of how things work, you can't even reliably cross a street without endangering your life. Your whole existence becomes a series of interesting guesses.

Bill Bryson, *Neither Here Nor There*, HarperCollins, New York 1992, pp. 13, 15–16, 34–36

6. One of your German friends finds the book in your room. His attention is drawn by the book's cover. As he does not speak English, he asks you what it is about. **Outline** the book's content on the basis of the given excerpt.

7. **Write** your own travelogue about a recent trip you made and describe how you felt. Referring to Bryson's quote, what would you say was the "greatest reward and luxury" of travel if there is any.

M3 The Beach

Alex Garland/John Hodge

The Beach (2000) is an adventure drama film based on the novel (1996) of the same name by Alex Garland. The film stars Leonardo DiCaprio who plays twenty-something Richard, an American backpacker with a love for world travel. Driven by the desire to seek and find adventures, Richard arrives in Bangkok, Thailand, where he will soon discover that the paradise that he set out to find is far from perfect.

Backpacker Richard in *The Beach* (2000)

1. What's the difference between a 'tourist' and a 'traveller'. Discuss this subject with a partner and compare your initial thoughts with the illustration below.

2. **Outline** the situation Richard finds himself in and **describe** the setting.

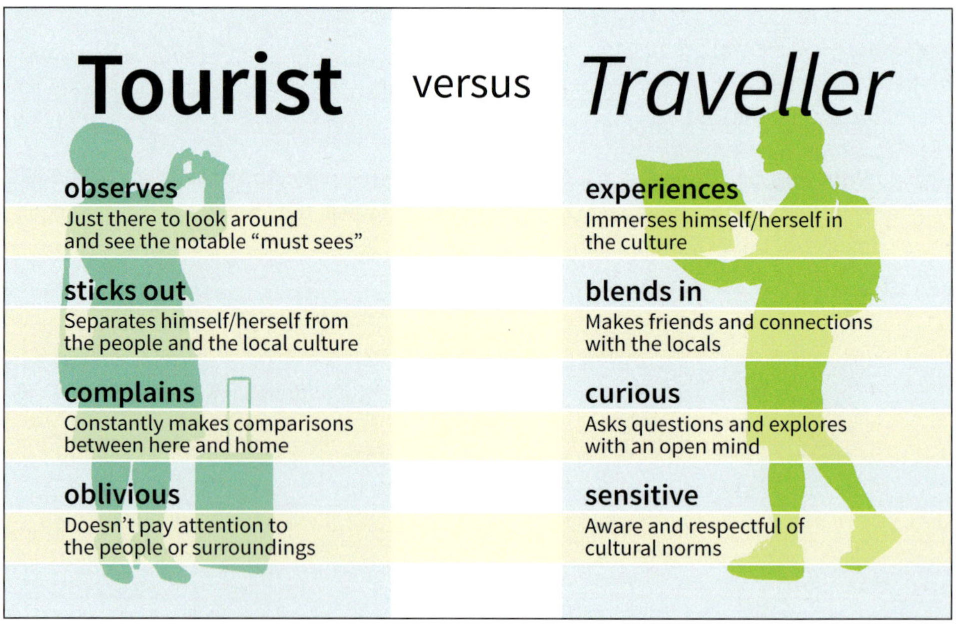

3. **Examine** what the conversations between the hustlers and Richard reveal about Bangkok and its people's attitude towards Westerners.

4. **Explain** why the statement by Traveler 4 in l. 72 is paradoxical.

5. Later in the film, Richard is being interviewed by a detective. In reply to the question whether he is a "tourist", Richard stresses that he is a "traveller". **Contrast** both terms on the basis of the given extract.

1. EXT. BANGKOK. NIGHT.
A single headlamp in close up shines directly and brightly out.
Extreme noise and light.
Beyond its glare can be seen the outline of a motorized tricycle ("tuk-tuk") and its Thai driver.
A young man, Richard, sits in the back, his rucksack beside him, swaying* with the motion of the vehicle. He is worn* and sweating.
They travel through nocturnal* Bangkok: fleets of tuk-tuks, taxis, road works, food vendors, dogs, tourists.
Music and credits.

2. EXT. KHAO SAN ROAD. NIGHT
The bright headlight comes to a halt.
Richard climbs down from the tuk-tuk.
RICHARD (V.O.)
When you hit Bangkok, there's really only one place to go.
The street is busy, full of Thais and travelers.
Richard picks his way through the crowd, his rucksack on his back.
He absorbs the scene as he passes boarding houses and hotels, and the shops and stalls selling food, clothes, pirated tapes, jewellery, travel tickets, and international phone calls.
Restaurants are filled with western travelers watching American films or European sport.
RICHARD (V.O.)
(continuing)
The Khao San Road is a decompression chamber between east and west. It's where you learn to breathe car fumes and tropical air for the very first time, or else carefully rearrange your memories before you catch your flight home.
Richard is approached by a young male Thai Hustler* who walks backwards in front of him while making his pitch*.
HUSTLER
You need somewhere to stay?
RICHARD
I'll be OK, Thanks.
Richard politely ignores each of his subsequent offers.
HUSTLER
What do you want? Sell your passport? Buy passport? Airline tickets? You want silk? I'll take you to the best silk place? You get a suit in twenty-four hours. Diamonds? You want to come with me, you get present for your girlfriend. Maybe no girlfriend. You want a girl, no problem. Good time. Boy girl fucking no problem. You want to drink some snake blood?
At this last one Richard stops and addresses the Hustler.
RICHARD
No thanks.
Richard walks on, the hustler fading out behind him.

EXT. exterior, *here:* outside, not in a building

to sway to move up and down
worn exhausted
nocturnal happening at night

V. O. voice-over, the voice of a person that cannot be seen speaking

hustler swindler

to make a pitch to attempt to sell sth.

to sip to drink small mouthfuls
Budweiser American beer

INT. interior, *here:* inside a building

rip off sth. not worth the amount paid

unspoiled natural and beautiful

off the beaten track far from main roads and towns; places where few people have been before

HUSTLER
You want designer clothes? I get you Versace, Gucci, Armani, no problem. You want a camera, all the best makes: Nikon, Leica, Canon I can get you.
RICHARD (V.O.)
Yeah, it's all here: you can phone home, meet up with strangers, split up with your friends, watch Hollywood movies while you sip Budweiser* and eat a burger or get some massage and green chicken soup. You could be anywhere in the world but you could only find it here. And what do they want, all these people?*

3. EXT. KHAO SAN ROAD. NIGHT./INT. BARS AND SHOPS. NIGHT.
Various young travelers, male and female, in snapshots excerpts, address their comments to the camera or each other.
TRAVELER 1
Where you been?
TRAVELER 2
Where you going?
TRAVELER 3
I've been there.
TRAVELER 4
It's a waste of time.
TRAVELER1
We just got back.
TRAVELER2
Fantastic.
TRAVELER 3
How much did it cost?
TRAVELER5
A complete rip off.*
TRAVELER3
Too many people. There's a much better place along the coast.
TRAVELER 4
We're going exploring. We've read this book. It tells us all the best places to explore.
TRAVELER 2
I know a place that everyone says is really unspoiled.*
TRAVELER 1
I heard they built a big hotel there.
TRAVELER 5
Some sort of sewage problem, apparently.
TRAVELER 1
We're going anyway: all the rooms have got air conditioning.
RICHARD (V.O.)
But for me it's all about finding out something about a place, and something about yourself. And when you get off the beaten track, that's where you find out what there is to find out.*
Richard turns into one of the restaurants.

Alex Garland/John Hodge, "The Beach", www.imsdb.com [02.01.2016]

M 4 Volunteering – Answers to the Questions of Being?

In recent years, a huge demand has evolved for going abroad programmes. There are programs which are often run by government bodies but in recent times many options have also come up in the private sector. Going abroad has become a prosperous industry. The question arises whether this development is part of an urge to 'polish up' one's CV or whether there is more to it. Do volunteers try to find answers to the core questions of their own identity?

1. Why do people spend their holidays working in other countries? Would you consider doing that in your next holidays? Develop a survey in which you try to find out about people's motives for going abroad and present your findings in graphs. Be prepared to present your results.

2. **Describe** the people on the next page. How is volunteering presented in these pictures?

3. Do further research on programs in Germany which offer the chance of going abroad. Choose one of the programs and develop a profile for it. Be prepared to present your profile to the class. In the profile, consider the following aspects:
   - The aims of the program
   - Steps to organize before and after going abroad, and in regard to the journey.
   - Financing your trip
   - Additional packages which are offered within the program

Zoom in: Skills

Developing a Survey

Aims:

When doing a survey, you want to find out what many people (of a certain group) think about a certain topic. For example, you can compare what students and teachers at your school think about volunteering abroad. In order to get the information, you need to observe the following steps:

Finding a topic:

The need for a survey usually arises out of a topic that you have worked on. Use your knowledge on that topic to specify the information you want to gain. Ask yourself what results you want the survey to produce.

Preparing the survey:

- Collect all the questions which come to your mind when thinking about the topic.
- Group all the questions which tend in the same direction.
- Choose the most relevant questions.
- Keep in mind: the fewer questions you have, the more likely it is that they will be answered.
- Use clear and simple language so that the reader immediately understands the question.
- Choose the type of answers which you need (multiple choice, scales, absolute numbers or free answers).
- On the basis of your assumptions, develop possible answers to the questions (unless you want open questions with free answers).
- Avoid redundant or very similar answers.

Conducting the survey:
- Decide who should be part of your survey group.
- Decide on how to introduce the survey to the people you want to ask. (What do you explain? How do you explain it?)
- Collect your data and ask only one question at a time.

Assessment:
- Analyse the data you collected.
- Prepare a visual presentation of your data (e.g. graphs, charts, mind maps for free answers)
- In your presentation, present your survey questions as well as the most relevant results.

Adapted and taken from: "Grafstat Software", www.bpb.de [01.01.2016]

German volunteers in a Chinese bakery shop preparing traditional biscuits together (Wuhan, China, December 2013)

Dell Volunteers support a project in Austin, Texas

A volunteer at the Cheetah Conservation Fund (CCF), South Africa

M 5 The Good, the Bad and the Ugly of Volunteer Travel

Danielle Marr

Danielle Marr is in her twenties and loves travelling. She writes articles for the digital magazine *Honest Blue*, which was founded in April 2013 by Hillside Media in Britain. According to the description on their website, *Honest Blue* "covers, analyses, comments on, and defines the news, culture, entertainment, fashion, and personalities that drive green, hipster lifestyles."

1. Look at the title of the given article and make an educated guess on what might be "the Good" as well as "the Bad and the Ugly" of volunteer work. Discuss in buzz groups.

2. After having read the introduction (ll. 1–17), split the class in half with one group reading "The Good" (ll. 18–51) and one "The Bad and The Ugly" (ll. 52–89). **Point out** the author's arguments for or respectively against volunteer work to a partner from the opposing group.

3. Together, **compare** the arguments and **evaluate** them according to their relevance.

4. The essayist T. S. Eliot once said: *"Most of the evil in this world is done by people with good intentions."* **Comment** on the quote and **discuss** whether the arguments against "voluntourism" outweigh the positive aspects.

The concept of voluntourism is exactly as the word implies – volunteering while travelling – and it can be an absolutely fantastic way to experience the world. While organizations like the Peace Corps have been around since 1961, the industry of volunteer travel has blossomed* since the 1990s, and now is a niche in and of itself.

to blossom to flourish

Nowadays if you do some quick googling, you will find hundreds of different organizations all over the world that can set you up with a volunteer project doing just about anything. Health initiatives, educational initiatives, eco projects, working with animals, building homes, working in orphanages ... you name it ... somewhere in the world, there is a demand for an extra set of helping hands. In fact, the wealth of information and potential projects to work with that you will find on the World Wide Web can be downright overwhelming. Unfortunately, however, there are a lot of projects out there that exist for all of the wrong reasons.

The same principle applies to those who seek out a place to volunteer abroad. While most begin their search with good intentions, it is important to look for a volunteer opportunity for the right reasons and to make sure that you choose a credible* organization to dedicate your time to. So here is an overview on why volunteer travel can be awesome and why it can be better to opt out* at times [...]

credible believable, trustworthy

to opt out to choose not to be part of sth.

THE GOOD

*Cultural Immersion**

immersion the state of being completely involved in sth.

Finding a place to volunteer in a foreign country can allow you to experience life somewhere in a way that you never would on your average vacation. It allows you to work directly with the locals and learn about the culture from those that live it every day rather than from a tour guide. Particularly if you find a place to volunteer that offers the opportunity to live in a homestay, you will be fully immersed in the local language, food and the lifestyle.

Making a Positive Impact

The number one reason that most people decide to volunteer abroad is so that they can make a positive impact on the place that they are visiting. If you can find a great, credible organization to work with and give yourself enough time to truly commit to a project, you CAN make a difference and it can be unbelievably rewarding. When you see a concept click in the eyes of one of your students or lay the last brick in a building project, you will know what I mean!

Increased International Awareness

beneficial having good effects

Experiencing something first hand will always be more beneficial* to you than reading it in a book or watching a documentary about it. Volunteering in developing countries can give you a much better sense of understanding of how the people there truly live, the struggles that they face on a daily basis and how they view their place in the world.

to bulk up sth. to make sth. bigger or more powerful

Bulk up your Résumé*

If you're not quite sure what you want to do with your life and are trying to decide on a new career path but lack experience, volunteering abroad can be a great option. It will help you gain practical experience as well as making you stand out in a crowd of other potential applicants. There is a whole pile of reasons as to why travelling and working abroad can make you a very unique job candidate, particularly if you find somewhere to volunteer that relates to your chosen field of study or work.

Economically Friendly Way To Travel

While this should most certainly not be your primary motivator in looking for a volunteer position, in some cases it can save you a ton of money while travelling. Many organizations will set you up with accommodation and food in exchange for your services (either for free or at an extremely low cost). So this means that the only money you will be spending would be on 'non-essential' aspects of your lifestyle (i. e. if you like to shop, party, or go for day trips around the area on your time off). [...]

THE BAD & THE UGLY

Volunteering For The Wrong Reasons

As I mentioned above, volunteering abroad can save you money. Unfortunately there are a lot of people who go into it with this as a sole motivator. So if this is you, just don't bother! Work for a few extra months at home to save and just go on a vacation. Another questionable reason for engaging in voluntourism is to do it for the purpose of a guilt free vacation. If you plan on volunteering for two days teaching at a school or working at an orphanage in the middle of a vacation for the sake* of giving yourself a pat on the back*, it is probably better to just opt out. Imagine having a new teacher or babysitter every day as a kid ... would you really think that any of them truly cared about you?

for the sake of because of/for the purpose of sth.
to give yourself a pat on the back to praise yourself

Coming Out Of It Disillusioned

This is where doing your research and choosing something and somewhere that you are truly passionate about comes into play. Oftentimes a volunteer project will sound cool and rewarding. But, if the organization doesn't really have much for you to do and just wants your money, if your skill set doesn't match the project terribly well, or if you don't speak the language and thus will struggle with even the simplest communication – it can be a recipe for coming home with a very deflated* ego and wondering why you went in the first place.

deflated feeling less positive/confident than before

Exploitation

There is a ton of information on the web about volunteer organizations exploiting both the communities they work with, as well as the volunteers they hire. It is a very extensive, sensitive topic. They can be taking jobs away from the local community, using the children of orphanages as commodities* to draw in more volunteers (and in turn, of course,

commodity *here*: material

more money) and taking the money they receive from donations for personal use rather than using it for its intended purpose. It is a very sad story, but a very common one.

Negative Psychological Effects

Oftentimes people will plan to go to a rural* community in a country that they know nothing about in hopes of 'making a difference' for a week. This speaks to the idea of volunteering for the wrong reasons, particularly when it comes to teaching or working in an orphanage. These children are extremely fragile* as it is. Having a westerner come in for a few days or a week to teach or play with them, only to up and leave again and experiencing this desertion* over, and over again will cause much more harm than good and will send the message that they are disposable. They need consistency and, at the very least, people who are relatively informed about the history and development of their country and thus understand their needs. It should primarily be the responsibility of the organization to properly screen potential volunteers and set a minimum time frame for which they accept volunteers. But, it is also your responsibility to do your research and make sure that you are dedicating your time to a reputable* and trustworthy cause.

Danielle Marr, "The Good, the Bad and the Ugly of Volunteer Travel", http://honestblue.com, 14.11.2013 [27.12.2015]

rural connected with the countryside

fragile easily broken

desertion abandonment

reputable respectable, well thought of

M 6 Responsible Volunteering Abroad Is the New Ideal

Volker Poelzl

Born and raised in Salzburg, Austria, Volker Poelzl is an experienced traveller and volunteer who has visited and lived in more than 30 countries worldwide. His passion for writing and travelling has made him a successful travel writer. His work has been published in the magazine *Transitions Abroad*. The magazine aims to provide information on the subject of working, studying, volunteering and living abroad. It supports individual travel instead of mass tourism. In one of the first editions of the magazine *Transitions Abroad* in 1977, a young traveller defined the difference between travellers and tourists as follows:

"Travelers and tourists, the distinction is simple: Tourists are those who bring their homes with them wherever they go, and apply them to whatever they see. They are closed to experiences outside of the superficial. Travelers, however, leave home at home, bringing only themselves and a desire to learn."

(Gary Langer, 1977, www.transitionsabroad.com [31.12.15])

1. Consider the distinction between travellers and tourists given in the quote above. To what extent do you agree with the statement and where do you see differences? Where would you place an international volunteer in relation to a tourist and a traveller?

2. **Explain** the newly coined word 'voluntourism'.

3. **Point out** benefits but also problems of voluntourism.

4. The title states that 'responsible volunteering abroad is the new ideal'. **Discuss** whether this is an appropriate compromise. Also consider whether the same title can be applied when it comes to voluntourism.

humanitarian aid projects *humanitäre Hilfsprojekte*

vacations holidays

ever-evolving continuously developing

to interact *sich gegenseitig beeinflussen*

mutual *gegenseitig*

immersed deeply involved, engaged, preoccupied

reputable respectable, worthy of respect

commitment involvement/engagement

Not too long ago international volunteer opportunities were largely limited to humanitarian aid projects* by churches, non-governmental organizations (NGOs), international government aid projects such as the *Peace Corps*, and large private sending organizations. Subsequently, there was a considerable change, as a growing number of people worldwide became interested in short-term volunteering, often in response to natural disasters around the world, but also as a way to combine travel with volunteer service. To meet the increasing demand, there have arrived an ever-growing number of volunteer organizations offering short-term volunteer vacations*. Also known as "voluntourism," these programs are attractive packages to many idealistic people of all ages, combining service work with adventure travel, language study, safaris, ecotourism, and more. However, ethical issues relating to this form of volunteering are being debated by some critics who have long worked in the field and question the effectiveness of certain volunteer vacations for the local community. In response, many volunteer sending organizations are taking into greater account the ever-evolving* ideals of responsible volunteering. Some critics are so strongly motivated by their ethical values and critiques that they see even the contributions of professional aid workers as an insertion of Western values in local communities with unintentional consequences.

[...] Generally, short-term volunteers are well taken care of during their vacations and are often assured of all the creature comforts demanded by many travelers. Activities are often, but not always, relatively pleasant and easy. No special language or job skills are required, and volunteers are assisted by local coordinators. In contrast to ordinary vacation packages, volunteer vacations give participants the opportunity to interact* with the locals and gain insight into their culture and way of life, while performing light work for several days or weeks at a time.

Of course, the contributions as part of a well-managed program may be important in a significant way to the local community. The money brought by voluntourists is often quite welcome in itself, and the intercultural relations and often results in mutually* beneficial relationships for all involved. Many short-term volunteers become so immersed* in their contributions that they seek out other longer-term volunteer work as a result, and the more skills they develop over time, the more valuable their help, even in training locals to continue the process on their own in a manner the local population deems most appropriate.

[...] While it is a very positive development that a growing number of travelers are seeking meaningful ways to spend their vacation time and money, it is important to be realistic about the benefits of short-term volunteer work. [...] Many well-established and reputable* referral organizations require a minimum commitment* of at least three weeks, simply because it takes at least that long to become familiar with and be integrated into an aid project in order to contribute substantially. In short, training takes valuable time and resources, much of which may be available in the local community already, with merely funds lacking.

Well-managed short-term help from volunteer vacationers certainly provides some very legitimate benefits to local communities, but participation is often limited to simple tasks. Not long ago in Guatemala I talked to an American expatriate, who is part of a small organization providing support and supplies for special education needs in the Guatemalan highlands. There were several international volunteers at his restaurant one evening, and we were discussing volunteer work and its benefits. He pointed out that short-term volunteers are little more than unskilled workers, doing simple tasks easily performed by the

locals. "What we don't have here is a shortage of labor, especially unskilled labor," he told me. "We don't really need foreign volunteers to come down here to lay bricks." His argument brings up the question of how much aid projects actually benefit from short-term, foreign participants, who come for a week to lay bricks, plant trees, or visit an orphanage for a few days.
[...] While the benefits of short-term volunteer work for local communities may be modest in some cases, there are nonetheless often many positive long-term effects. [...] Volunteer vacations provide travelers with the opportunity to get off the beaten path*, meet local people, and learn about their daily lives and rituals. Volunteers learn from their experience, and bring back such knowledge to their home communities. Knowledge helps participants to contribute to a better understanding and respect for foreign cultures and people, allows them to share their experiences and inspire others interested in volunteering, and most importantly continue to carry on and expand such new skills and learning at home.
[...]

Volker Poelzl, "Responsible Volunteering Abroad is the New Ideal", www.transitionsabroad.com, März 2015 [15.09.2015]

to get off the beaten path to take a route where not many people have been before

M7 Beware the 'Voluntourists' Doing Good

Ossob Mohamud

Ossob Mohamud is a Somalian blogger and journalist who writes for 'Africa on the Blog'. Some of her work has been published in *The Guardian*. Born in Doha, Qatar, she was raised both in Qatar as well as in Arlington, Virginia. She graduated with a degree in International Politics. She states that she has a major interest in postcolonial theory because she feels that it explains current global problems.

1. Voluntourism is a blend of the words 'volunteering' and 'tourism'. Develop a word field with both terms and include more synonyms and idioms which are connected to either 'tourism' or 'volunteering' or to both (e.g. travelling, (to) volunteer, to visit sights, to gain experience, to explore, etc.).
2. According to the Oxford Dictionary, voluntourism is "a form of tourism in which travellers participate in voluntary work" (www.oxforddictionaries.com [05.01.2016]). Compare this definition with the title of the article and take an educated guess as to what the message of the article may be.
3. **Outline** the problems of 'voluntourism' as shown by the author.
4. **Analyse** the author's attitude by **examining** her choice of words.
5. **Comment on** the author's statement that privileged people from developed countries are trying to overcome the "vacuity of modernity and globalization" (l. 40) by participating in voluntourism. State your opinion and provide justification for your position.

I recently came across an interesting article questioning voluntourism and assessing whether it does more harm than good in communities of the global south*. It reminded me of my own concerns with "voluntourism" that originated in my college years in which I had participated in Alternative Spring Breaks. It was considered an alternative to what most college students did on their vacations: spending idle time by the poolside. The

global south southern hemisphere, countries which are supposedly less developed than countries of the northern hemisphere

poverty-stricken troubled by poverty

interspersed intermixed

disingenuous *unaufrichtig, arglistig*

condescending arrogant

benevolent kind, helpful

alleviation relief, reduction

to cringe *erschaudern*

to spruce up to polish up, to improve

to sprout to grow

to assuage [ə'sweɪdʒ] to make sth. less severe

redemption penance, atonement

to atone *für etw. büßen, wieder gutmachen*

vacuity emptiness

university-organised trips sent students to spend a week in disadvantaged and poverty-stricken* communities to volunteer. This could take the form of teaching English at the local school, assisting in building and beautifying new homes for residents, or environmental clean-ups. Interspersed* throughout the week were also touristy getaways and souvenir shopping. Although I had memorable and rewarding moments, I could never shake off the feeling that it was all a bit too self-congratulatory and disingenuous*.

Voluntourism almost always involves a group of idealistic and privileged travelers who have vastly different socio-economic statuses vis-à-vis those they serve. They often enter these communities with little or no understanding of the locals' history, culture, and ways of life. All that is understood is the poverty and the presumed neediness of the community, and, for the purposes of volunteering, that seems to be enough. In my own experiences – also highlighted by the author of the article – this has led to condescending* and superficial relationships that transform the (usually western) volunteer into a benevolent* giver and the community members into the ever grateful receivers of charity. It makes for an extremely uncomfortable dynamic in which one begins to wonder if these trips are designed more for the spiritual fulfillment of the volunteer rather than the alleviation* of poverty.

I couldn't help feeling ashamed at the excessive praise and thanks we received from locals and those on the trip alike. I cringed* as we took complimentary photos with African children whose names we didn't know. We couldn't even take full credit for building the houses because most of the work had already been done by community members. In fact, if anything we slowed down the process with our inexperience and clumsiness. And how many schools in the west would allow amateur college students to run their English classes for a day? What had I really done besides inflate my own ego and spruce* up my resume? I had stormed into the lives of people I knew nothing about, I barely engaged with them on a genuine level, and worst of all, I then claimed that I had done something invaluable for them all in a matter of five days (of which most of the time was spent at hotel rooms, restaurants, and airports).

An entire industry has sprouted* out of voluntourism as it increases in popularity, possibly equal to the increase in global inequality. As the gap between rich and poor widens, so too it seems does the need for those of the global north to assuage* the guilt of their privilege (paradoxically, guilt only seems to deepen as many realise the illusory effect of their impact), or to simply look good. The developing world has become a playground for the redemption* of privileged souls looking to atone* for global injustices by escaping the vacuity* of modernity and globalisation.

A volunteer working with local children in Kenya

But does this address the root institutional and structural causes of the problem? I do not mean to deny, across the board, the importance of the work voluntourists do. Volunteers in developing countries fund and deliver great programmes that would not happen otherwise, but the sustainability and the effectiveness of the approach is what I question. Time and energy would be better spent building real solidarity between disparate* societies based on mutual respect and understanding. Instead of focusing on surface symptoms of poverty, volunteers and the organisations that recruit them should focus on the causes that often stem from* an unjust global economic order. Why not advocate and campaign for IMF and World Bank reforms? How about having volunteers advocate for their home country to change aggressive foreign and agricultural policies (such as subsidy programmes)? This might seem unrealistic but the idea is to get volunteers to understand their own (direct or indirect) role in global poverty. The idea is to get volunteers truly invested in ending poverty, and not simply to feel better about themselves.

Ossob Mohamud, "Beware the 'Voluntourists' Doing Good", www.africanontheblog.com/on-voluntourism-2, 13.02.2013 [24.09.2015]

disparate different, unequal, divergent

to stem from to be the result of sth.

M 8a Interview with Carrie Hessler-Radelet, Director of the Peace Corps

Greg Hubbs, John Dwyer

The following interview between the editors of *Transitions Abroad*, Greg Hubbs and John Dwyer, and Carrie Hessler-Radelet, director of the Peace Corps, was published on 5 November 2015. Hessler-Radelet is the 19th director of the Peace Corps and was sworn in on 25 June 2014. Her family has been involved with the Peace Corps for four generations, and this initially led to her decision to become a Peace Corps volunteer in Western Samoa from 1981–1983. She used the experience gained there in her later work as director of the institution.

1. **Outline** the aims of the Peace Corps as shown in the interview.

2. **Explain** Hessler-Radelet's idea of the term 'global citizens' (ll. 50 f.).

3. **Comment on** whether the ideal of 'responsible volunteering' as shown in M 6 can be applied to the Peace Corps. Give reasons for your position.

Greg Hubbs: At a conference on December 9, 2014 hosted by the White House [...] – where there was a concerted* and clearly coordinated effort by the Administration to increase the quantity and diversity of young Americans going abroad for many reasons ranging from educational to humanitarian to diplomatic to economic and more ... – you mentioned that the Peace Corps is one volunteer assignment where you can enter the force "broke" and walk away with a stipend* after service. You also suggested that it is a great way to learn languages and gain cultural experience. The experience sounded so life-changing that we wished that we could join on the spot!

Since the prevailing view in the volunteer field is that the most effective volunteers are those who can bring some tangible skills to the table, what qualifications and personality characteristics do you look for in a Peace Corps candidate and how would any individual looking to sign up know that they are realistically a good candidate?

concerted sth. is done in a planned and determined way

stipend scholarship, salary

Carrie Hessler-Radelet

diversity *Vielfalt*
minority participation participants are part of a minority group in the U.S.

to serve to work as a volunteer

perseverance *Ausdauer, Durchhaltevermögen*

Carrie Hessler-Radelet: Peace Corps service is highly competitive, and we're looking for applicants with a college degree and a commitment to serve others. Volunteers come from all walks of life and have a broad range of skill sets and career priorities. Some potential volunteers will be interested in a specific area of the world, others in a specific language, program, or sector area. Flexibility, an open mind and a willingness to learn are strong qualities that make successful volunteers. [...]

G. H.: What sort of training do you provide?

Carrie Hessler-Radelet: The Peace Corps provides volunteers with thorough and comprehensive training so they can have a safe and productive volunteer experience. Once invitees have accepted their Peace Corps assignment, we provide online training materials and country-specific information. When volunteers arrive in a country, they participate in pre-service training, which includes about three months of intensive cultural, language, safety and technical training. Volunteers often stay with host families during this period to help them integrate into their communities. After being sworn into service and moving to permanent sites, volunteers continue to receive formal training and support from in-country Peace Corps staff throughout their service.

G. H.: You spoke at the conference about the importance now being placed on both diversity* of destination and diversity of minority participation*. You said that you were proud of the more than 60 countries, and growing, in which the Peace Corps operates and that 25 % of volunteers are now minorities. We are pleased to hear about the amount of diversity in the program. How have you managed to achieve such progress?

Carrie Hessler-Radelet: A diverse and inclusive environment is essential to achieving the Peace Corps mission. We are committed to ensuring the Peace Corps represents the rich diversity of the United States. We want every American to know about the Peace Corps, and we want to reflect the diversity of America in our volunteers abroad. Peace Corps' Office of Diversity and National Outreach aims to recruit a diverse pool of volunteers and build an inclusive culture that welcomes applicants and volunteers from all backgrounds. [...]

John Dwyer: How does the Peace Corps determine what type of volunteer skills are needed in the host countries?

Carrie Hessler-Radelet: Our volunteers serve* at the invitation of our host countries, and our staff works with host country governments to identify their needs and goals, and that guides the types of volunteer assignments we offer in each Peace Corps country. [...]

G. H.: We know that Returned Volunteers seem to have had disproportionate success in their careers. What do you think are the primary qualities carried forth from the volunteer experience that have enabled so many Returned Peace Corps Volunteers to become successful freelancers, entrepreneurs, and great leaders?

Carrie Hessler-Radelet: Peace Corps volunteers return home as global citizens with new perspectives. They have cross-cultural, leadership, language, teaching and community development skills that give them a competitive edge for advanced education and job opportunities in today's global economy. They also develop vital life skills, such as perseverance* and flexibility, and get hands-on program management experience. In our interconnected world, these are vital skills that employers are looking for now more than ever. The unique Peace Corps experience helps returned volunteers find success across a number of fields and industries, and many continue their service in their local communities. [...]

Greg Hubbs, John Dwyer, "Interview with Carrie Hessler-Radelet", www.transitionsabroad.com, 11.05.2015 [15.09.2015]

Zoom in: Terminology

The **Peace Corps** is a volunteering program which is run by the government of the United States of America. Its mission is to "promote world peace and friendship" (www.peacecorps.gov) by offering skilled help to interested countries and thereby enabling mutual understanding of each other's culture.

The Peace Corps was founded by President John F. Kennedy in March 1961 with the aim of promoting international development and cross-cultural exchange. The program was quickly approved so that the first Peace Corps volunteers soon left for Ghana, Tanzania and Nigeria. The organisation grew rapidly and, by 1966, 15,000 volunteers were serving in the field.

Official logo of the US Peace Corps

Faced with declining participation, President Barack Obama enabled a large financial package in Congress for the Peace Corps. Since then, the Peace Corps missions have been reorganized and improved with new initiatives.

Applicants must be at least 18 years old and have American citizenship. The volunteers typically have a secondary education in the form of a college degree. The aim is to serve two years in the field as a volunteer. There are also programs for qualified professionals serving on short-term assignments. Assignments can take place in the areas of education, health, the environment, and agriculture as well as in the field of the economic development of a community.

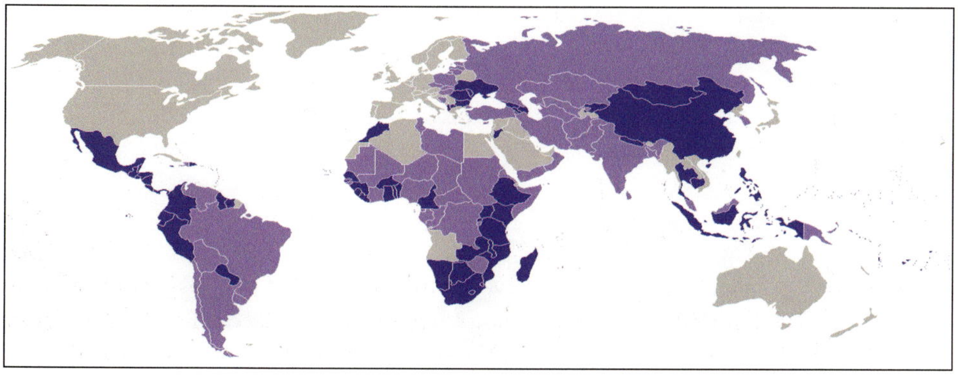

Countries which the Peace Corps has served in up until 2009 are presented in light blue and countries which the Peace Corps has been serving in since 2009 in dark blue.

4. Describe the map on recent developments in the Peace Corps. Prepare a 2-minute presentation about the Peace Corps, its aims and its global relevance on the basis of the map and with the help of the given information on the institution in the info box above.

Zoom in: Vocabulary

Talking about maps

- The map shows/depicts/illustrates/is about/gives information about ...
- The (light blue/grey/dark blue) areas stand for/represent ...
- Most/some of the (dark blue/light blue) areas are located in ...
- The map shows/depicts a high percentage of ... in ...
- There is a concentration of ... in the northern/southern hemisphere.

M 8b Be a Volunteer – Peace Corps Advertising Video

Peace Corps

This video was produced as a general advertisement for the Peace Corps programme. It was first shown on 1 September 2011 on YouTube as well as on the official website of the Peace Corps. It promotes the benefits of the Peace Corps as well as the experiences made available to the volunteers.

1. Keeping in mind the information about the Peace Corps which you read in the interview, what kind of advertising do you expect in the video?

@ SNG-40660-003

Viewing

2. Together with a partner, develop an interview with one of the volunteers after his/her mission has been completed. Focus on his/her initial aims in connection with his/her volunteering service and analyse them in relation to his/her development after his/her mission. Think of ways of demonstrating his/her possible personal growth and his/her goals for the future.

M 9 Grußworte zum Festakt des fünfjährigen Bestehens des Freiwilligendienstes des Auswärtigen Amtes „Kulturweit"

Frank-Walter Steinmeier

Kulturweit is a German volunteer program which is run by the Federal Foreign Office and enables young Germans between 18 and 25 to work as volunteers in foreign countries. The volunteers support German cultural institutions such as the Goethe-Institute, the German Academic Exchange Service (DAAD), German schools abroad (ZfA/PAD), the Deutsche Welle (Germany's international broadcasting institution) or the German archaeological institute. The young people can choose to stay abroad either for 6 or for 12 months. The program promotes cross-cultural experiences and supports intercultural learning by means of an effective and extensive course of training before, during and after a volunteer's stay.

ZOOM IN: People

Frank-Walter Steinmeier is a German lawyer and politician, who has been serving as Federal Minister of Foreign Affairs since 2013. He is a member of the Social Democratic Party and from 2009 to 2013 he was the party leader.
Steinmeier was born on 5 January 1956 in Detmold, North Rhine-Westphalia. He finished secondary school in 1974 and then completed two years of military service. Afterwards, he went on to obtain a law degree from the University of Gießen as well as a degree in political science. He graduated in 1982 and took his second state examination in law in 1986. He gained his doctorate in law in 1991 from the university of Gießen.
On completing his academic studies, Steinmeier started his political career in Hanover, Lower Saxony, and served as Undersecretary of State and as Director of the State Chancellery of Lower Saxony. During the Schröder government, he became Head of the Office of the Chancellor in 1999. He was also responsible for co-ordinating Germany's intelligence services.
After the federal election in 2005, he became Minister of Foreign Affairs in the Grand Coalition cabinet with Angela Merkel as chancellor. Two years later, he was made vice-chancellor. In 2008, it was decided that Steinmeier should run for the office of chancellor in the 2009 election. After losing the elections, he became leader of the parliamentary opposition.
Following on the 2013 elections, which resulted in another Grand Coalition, Steinmeier was again appointed Minister of Foreign Affairs and was, among other diplomatic issues, confronted with the conflict in the Ukraine as well as the war in Syria.

1. Imagine you attended the festivities marking the 5-year anniversary of *Kulturweit* as a journalist and listened to the following speech. You are working for a university magazine which is run by students. Your editor has asked you to **outline** the main points of Steinmeier's speech for the next edition in the English language.

@ SNG-40660-004

2. **Compare** the presentation of *Kulturweit* with the image given of the Peace Corps in its advertising video.

3. Do further research on *Kulturweit* and other German volunteering organizations for young people. Find out whether they all aim at spreading the idea of the 'shared view' as described by Steinmeier.

aus der Taufe heben to launch sth.

Mittlerorganisation intermediary organisations

Kulturbotschafter cultural ambassador

Streitschlichter mediator

den Blick erweitern to broaden one's view

Liebe Verena Metze-Mangold,
lieber Stephan Dorgerloh,
meine Damen und Herren,
und vor allem liebe „Kulturweit"-Alumni!

Als wir „Kulturweit" vor fünf Jahren aus der Taufe gehoben* haben, da war dieser neue Freiwilligendienst nur den wenigsten ein Begriff.

Wenn ich mich hier [...] umsehe, dann bietet sich ein anderes Bild. Offensichtlich hat sich herumgesprochen, dass wir hier heute Abend fünf Jahre „Kulturweit" feiern. Dieses „Kulturweit" hat sich etabliert.

Fünf Jahre „Kulturweit" – da ist ein Traum Wirklichkeit geworden. Liebe Frau Metze-Mangold, was wir uns 2009 gemeinsam mit den Partnern in den Mittlerorganisationen* ausgedacht haben, das hat – auch manchen Widrigkeiten zum Trotz – Gestalt angenommen.

Liebe Kulturweit-Alumni, das ist vor allem euer Verdienst! Bald 2 000 junge Leute sind in den letzten fünf Jahren als Kulturbotschafter* unseres Landes in alle Welt ausgeschwärmt. In über siebzig Ländern sind „Kulturweit"-Freiwillige am Werk.

Ob sie als Lehrerin im serbischen Subotica, als Jungarchäologen in Istanbul oder bei der UNESCO in Mexiko Stadt gearbeitet haben – ihr Elan ist nicht mehr aus unserer Auswärtigen Kultur- und Bildungspolitik wegzudenken.

Worum es „Kulturweit" im Kern geht, das hat vor zwei Wochen der Schriftsteller Rajivinder Singh auf den Punkt gebracht, als er mich auf meine Reise nach Indien begleitet hat. Unterwegs im Flugzeug hat er von einer auswärtigen Kulturpolitik der sechs Augen gesprochen:

Wir sollen die Welt mit unseren Augen sehen, mit denen unserer Freunde – und mit einem gemeinsamen Blick. Ich finde das eine treffende Aufgabenbeschreibung für Außenpolitik insgesamt, aber auch für das, worauf es „Kulturweit" ankommt.

Wie unerlässlich das ist, das erleben wir gerade heute in einer ganz neuen Dringlichkeit. Wir spüren das in der Ukraine-Krise, im Kampf gegen die Terroristen des Islamischen Staats, im Ringen um Frieden für den Nahen Osten. Wir merken es aber auch immer stärker im Alltag unserer immer enger vernetzten Welt.

Liebe Ehemalige, den Blick der sechs Augen haben viele von Ihnen während des „Kulturweit"-Jahrs eingeübt: als Streitschlichter* in Albanien, als Umwelt-Beraterin in Argentinien oder als Organisator einer Schreibwerkstatt in Weißrussland.

Damit haben Sie eben nicht nur Ihren Blick auf die Welt geweitet*. Mit Ihrem Engagement wird sich diese Welt auch ein bisschen verändern – und ich glaube zum Besseren. Darauf können Sie stolz sein.

Im August 2009 ist Valentin Schmehl als einer der ersten „Kulturweit"-Freiwilligen nach Bethlehem gereist. Er hat dort als Volontär in einem Internat für Kinder mit schwierigem familiärem Hintergrund gearbeitet. Über diese eindringliche Erfahrung hat er einige Monate später geschrieben:

„Die Hälfte des interkulturellen Kuchens ist gegessen. Satt bin ich noch lange nicht, und das Verdauen wird noch einige Zeit in Anspruch nehmen."

Ich glaube, diese Worte sprechen vielen hier aus der Seele, denen „Kulturweit" Lust auf mehr Engagement gemacht hat. Deshalb ist es eine großartige Nachricht, dass es jetzt Pläne gibt, einen Alumni-Verein zu gründen.

Deshalb freue ich mich besonders, dass wir in diesem Sommer eine schmerzhafte Kürzung des „Kulturweit"-Etats haben abwenden können. Und deshalb wollen wir uns in den nächsten Jahren gemeinsam dafür einsetzen, dass dieses einzigartige Projekt weitergeht und weiter gedeiht!

Frank-Walter Steinmeier, „Grußworte zum Festakt des fünfjährigen Bestehens des Freiwilligendienstes des Auswärtigen Amtes ‚Kulturweit'", www.auswaertiges-amt.de, 17.09.2014 [07.09.2015]

M 10 Gap Years: Wasted Youth?

Patrick Kingsley

Journalist Patrick Kingsley travelled to the resort of Had Rin on the island of Koh Phangan in Thailand, a popular gap year resort, to meet backpackers attending the infamous Full Moon Party.

Full Moon Party in Thailand, bucket vendors

1. **Outline** how modern backpackers spend their gap year according to Kingsley.
2. **Point out** why, as reported by Mary Curnock Cock, Richard Oliver, and Hans Hoefer, this poses a problem.
3. **Explain** the ambiguity of the article's title.
4. **Examine** the choice of words that is used to characterize the "gappers" travelling to Thailand's Full Moon Party.
5. **Illustrate** by which means Kingsley convinces the readers of his opinion.
6. The article states that school-leavers should use their gap years in more "constructive" ways (l. 24). Against the backdrop of what you have learned so far, **discuss** the potential options for such a constructive gap year experience.

Up and down the beach, young western men are unzipping their shorts and peeing into the Gulf of Thailand. Behind them, under the light of the full moon, thousands more

generic *gleichförmig*
stall a small shop or counter
to daub *beschmieren, bemalen*
lurid unpleasantly shocking
moronic very stupid

Banana Pancake Trail metaphor for places in Southeast Asia that are popular among Western tourists
epitome embodiment
pinnacle the highest point of achievement

to dwarf to make sth. seem small

to trickle down to spread slowly

hedonism ['hedənɪzəm] lifestyle of pure enjoyment

to binge to drink an excessive amount of alcohol

lure attraction

crammed packed full
to blare out to sing loudly
hawker person who sells goods aggressively, often by calling out
to jostle to push and shove harshly

shirtless, shoeless Europeans are massed outside 14 beachside bars, their knees bending awkwardly to a soundtrack of the Black Eyed Peas, Justin Bieber and generic* drum'n'bass. And squeezed between the bars and the crowds are 35 wooden stalls*, each selling plastic buckets filled with a litre's worth of vodka and Red Bull. The stalls are daubed* with deeply dubious slogans, ranging from the lurid* to the moronic*. "No Bucket No Boom Boom", "Fuck My Buckets", "Everybody Fuck My Strong Buckets" – that kind of thing.

Welcome to the Full Moon Party, the largest beach rave in the world. Twenty-five years ago, this was a little-known hippy hang-out on the remote Thai island of Koh Phangan. Today, frequented every month by between 10,000 and 30,000 European youngsters, the all-night party is the ultimate destination on south-east Asia's "banana pancake" trail*; a mecca for footloose gap-year tourists. This party scene, right here on this beach, is arguably the epitome*, the pinnacle*, of the modern gap-year experience.

Three weeks ago, the chief executive of the universities and colleges admissions service (UCAS) declared to a Sunday newspaper that "the golden age of the gap year is over". Mary Curnock Cook argued that while in the past "a gap year has been when young people take a nice break and go out and see the world", the period should now "be used in a focused way to support an application to the course or university you are targeting". In a year when the number of university applications – a record 660,000 – has dwarfed* the number of university places available – 450,000 – Curnock Cook may have a point.

But this is a point that has yet to trickle down*, in practical terms, to the nation's school-leavers. In fact, the vast majority of gappers do not use their year-out in anything approaching a fashion that might – in the eyes of universities – be viewed as "constructive". Every year around 160,000 British school-leavers take a gap year before entering university. More than 80 % of them, says Richard Oliver, chairman of trustees at Year Out, "just go off and travel independently without any real purpose. Sun, sand and sangria, as I call it." Indeed, the trend might even be away from the year of constructive good deeds that Curnock Cook might be thinking of – a trend towards increasingly mindless hedonism*.

Hans Hoefer is the founder of *Insight travel books*, and the man who co-ordinated one of the first guides to Thailand back in the 70s, when fewer tourists visited the entire country (150,000) than now visit Burma annually. These days "gappers" touring Koh Phangan and its surrounding islands are, says Hoefer, "not experiencing anything apart from tourism. It's an absolute joke. They don't want to understand the culture – they just want to binge*. I don't understand why they go."

Attempting to understand why they go, however, why *this* is the modern gap-year experience, is exactly what brings me to the Full Moon Party, surrounded by scores of topless teenagers urinating into the ocean to the words of the Black Eyed Peas' "I gotta feeling/That tonight's gonna be a good night/That tonight's gonna be a good, good night." What exactly is the lure* of this beach to teenagers who are, after all, meant to be Britain's brightest? I'm here to find out.

When gappers touch down in Bangkok, their first port-of-call is almost always the backpackers' ghetto on the Khao San Road. In *The Beach*, Alex Garland's 1996 novel about a young man's search for adventure in Thailand, Khao San is described as a decompression chamber between east and west. But when I arrive, it soon becomes clear that even this is a generous description; the Khao San Road actually doesn't feel like it's in Thailand at all. The street is crammed* with bars showing premiership football; Britney Spears and Bob Dylan blare out* of every speaker; hawkers* selling European T-shirts jostle* with those selling fake British ID cards. This April, 20 Thais were massacred in clashes between soldiers and anti-government redshirt protesters barely 100 metres from the Khao San Road. But it might as well have been 100 miles away: the Khao San's tourist festivities were barely disrupted. And when Alex, a well-travelled graphic designer from west London who "took several gap years", muses to me that "the Khao San just feels like home", he's spot on, though perhaps not in quite the way he intends: apart from the fat, bald westerners parading their suspiciously beautiful Thai girlfriends, the road could be a carbon copy* of Camden High Street. [...]

Patrick Kingsley, "Gap Years: Wasted Youth?", www.theguardian.com, 06.09.2010 [01.02.2016]

carbon copy exact copy

M 11 Gringo Trails: Is Tourism Destroying the World?

Boyd Matson

In this broadcast, anchorman Boyd Matson interviews Pegi Vail and Melvin Estrella. Vail is an anthropologist and Associate Director of the Center for Media, Culture, and History at NYU (New York University). Furthermore, she is the director and producer of the feature-length documentary *Gringo Trails* which was released in 2013. Estrella co-produced the documentary and functioned as director of photography,

1. A famous Native American saying concerning travelling states: "Take nothing but memories, leave nothing but footprints." Do you agree? Why (not)?

2. The picture below shows a film still of the documentary *Gringo Trails* which was directed and produced by the American anthropologist Pegi Vail. Speculate about the title of the documentary as well as its contents.

Listening

3. **Outline**
   a) how tourism has changed.
   b) the pros and cons of people travelling.
   c) in what way the new kind of tourism affects locals.

@ SNG-40660-005

4. Do some more research on the documentary and **evaluate** the importance of Pegi Vail's and Melvin Estrella's work in your own words.

Koh Phangan beach in Thailand after a Full Moon Party

M 12 Kicking the Bucket List

Rebecca Mead

'To kick the bucket' is an informal idiom and means 'to die'. Its original meaning is associated with the killing of animals for food. They were hung from a wooden frame (the bucket), which they would kick as they were dying. A 'bucket list' is a catalogue or wish list documenting the things and places you want to do or see before you kick the bucket. In the following article, Rebecca Mead reflects upon the concept of having a bucket list.

1. Would you say keeping a bucket list is a worthwhile thing to do? If so, what would be on your bucket list? Exchange your views with a partner.
2. Considering the meaning of 'to kick the bucket', speculate about the title of the article and the author's intention in writing it.
3. **Sum up** in what ways it becomes evident that keeping a bucket list is quite popular nowadays.
4. **Explain** what the author means by the so-called "YOLO-ization of cultural experience".
5. **Evaluate** the author's view on "YOLO-ization" against the backdrop of your own experiences and goals.

Given the daunting* agenda of international crises – in Ukraine, Syria, Iraq – with which world leaders contended at the NATO summit* in Newport, Wales, last week, it is forgivable that President Obama chose to indulge* in a little cultural tourism before departing from the U.K. At the summit's close, the President had his helicopter stop by Boscombe Down Air Force Base in Wiltshire, so that he and his motorcade could make the twenty-minute drive to Stonehenge. He strode jacketless around the monument's weathered*, lichen-covered* stones, and listened earnestly to the site's English Heritage curator. "Knocked it off the bucket list right now," he told watching reporters before returning to his car and to Washington, an hour behind his official schedule.

The concept of the bucket list – places one wants to visit, experiences one wants to undergo, and accomplishments one wants to master before dying – has gained widespread cultural currency*, and that the President should talk of having one should not be surprising. [...]

Exactly who coined the phrase is obscure, but the term entered the popular consciousness decisively in 2007, with the release of the movie "The Bucket List." Starring Jack Nicholson and Morgan Freeman as geriatric* terminal-cancer patients who undertake an implausible valedictory* tour of excess – skydiving, visiting the Taj Mahal, and getting to the foothills of Everest. [...]

The idea rapidly spread to a younger generation: in 2010, MTV's "The Buried Life" featured three fresh-faced* Canadian guys travelling across America and checking items off their list, among them "Streak a stadium* and get away with it," "Throw the most badass party ever," and "Spend a night in jail."

The expression derives from "kicking the bucket," a euphemism* for dying of obscure origin but blunt* and vivid suggestiveness. [...]

Compiling a bucket list is both an exercise in wishful self-improvement – learning to speak French, training to run a marathon – and an expression of to-hell-with-it cupidity*. It can express the longing to shed inhibition, as if living life to its fullest meant dispensing

daunting frightening, alarming
The **2014 Wales summit** was held on 4 and 5 September 2014
to indulge to delight in, to relish, to give yourself a treat
weathered *verwittert*
lichen ['litʃən] tiny organisms growing on rocks and trees; *Flechte*
currency *here*: distribution
geriatric old, advanced in age
valedictory farewell
fresh-faced young
to streak a stadium to run across a stadium pitch naked
euphemism ['ju:fəmizəm] a pleasant name for something unpleasant
blunt straightforward
cupidity *Begierde, Habgier*

with socially constraining rules. The felicitous rhyme with "fuck it," the plosive "b" substituting for the fricative "f," surely goes part of the way to explaining the term's appeal. A small library could be filled with the books that have been written for those who feel their imaginations inadequate to the task of summoning a roster* of ambitions or desires. [e. g. Patricia Schultz's *1000 Places to See Before You Die ...*]

roster ['rɒstə] list

There are countless interactive tools for filling one's bucket or examining the contents of someone else's. The iWish app allows you to input your life goals – suggestions range from "Dive the Galapagos Islands" to "Raise a Happy & Healthy Child" – and have them always only a finger-swipe away. Bucketlist.org calls itself "a web-based personal intentions system"; its users can list their goals, post updates about their accomplishments, and evaluate the goals of other people. This last is voyeuristically fascinating and oddly poignant*: the two-hundred-and-ninety-five-goal list of one young woman in Hyderabad, which includes "Hand out lemons wearing a shirt that says life," "Look like a boy," "Do something I'm not supposed to," "Be surprised," and "Be unbelievably surprised," is a young-adult novel in note form. [...]

poignant ['pɔɪnjənt] melancholic

As popularly conceived, however, the bucket list is far from being a reckoning* with the weight of love in extremis, or an ethical or moral accounting. More often, it partakes* of a commodification of cultural experience, in which every expedition made, and every artwork encountered, is reduced to an item on a checklist to be got through, rather than being worthy of repeated or extended engagement. Dropping by Stonehenge for ten minutes and then announcing you've crossed it off your bucket list suggests that seeing Stonehenge – or beholding the Taj Mahal, or visiting the Louvre, or observing a pride of lions slumbering under a tree in the Maasai Mara – is something that, having been done, can be considered done with.

reckoning balance, settling of debts
to partake to become involved

This is the YOLO-ization* of cultural experience, whereby the pursuit of fleeting* novelty is granted greater value than a patient dedication to an enduring attention – an attention which might ultimately enlarge the self, and not just pad one's experiential résumé. The notion of the bucket list legitimizes this diminished* conception of the value of repeated exposure to art and culture. Rather, it privileges a restless consumption, a hungry appetite for the new. I've *seen* Stonehenge. Next?

YOLO acronym for 'you only live once'
fleeting brief, transient, short-lived
diminished limited, decreased, lesser

What if, instead, we compiled a different kind of list, not of goals to be crossed out but of touchstones to be sought out over and over, with our understanding deepening as we draw nearer to death? These places, experiences, or cultural objects might be those we can only revisit in remembrance – we may never get back to the Louvre – but that doesn't mean we're done with them. The greatest artistic and cultural works, like an unaccountable* sun rising between ancient stones, are indelible*, with the power to induce* enduring wonder if we stand still long enough to see.

unaccountable inexplicable
indelible permanent
induce cause

Rebecca Mead, "Kicking the Bucket List", www.newyorker.com, 11.09.2014 [29.12.2015] © Conde Nast

6. Think about the question raised by the author in ll. 59–63. What would your touchstones be? Write a personal list.

International Internships and Work Experience – a Must Have?

M 1a Statistics on Work Experience and Gap Years

YouGov

YouGov is an international, internet-based market research firm, headquartered in the UK, with operations in Europe, North America, the Middle East and the Asia-Pacific region. The following statistics provide you with information about employers' perceptions of entrants who have spent time overseas working or travelling. The survey was conducted from 20 to 26 July 2011 among 251 Human Resource professionals.

1. In order to gather experience, many students work for free in internships. Moreover, there are also some who even pay a lot of money for that privilege. Would you be willing to spend money in order to work for free?

2. **Present** the results of the statistics provided.

3. In how far have the given statistics changed your initial thoughts on the question whether you would be willing to pay for an internship. **Justify** your answer.

To what extent do you agree, or disagree, with the following statements?

q1. Taking a constructive gap year involving independent travel, working or volunteering overseas is a worthwhile experience for young people.

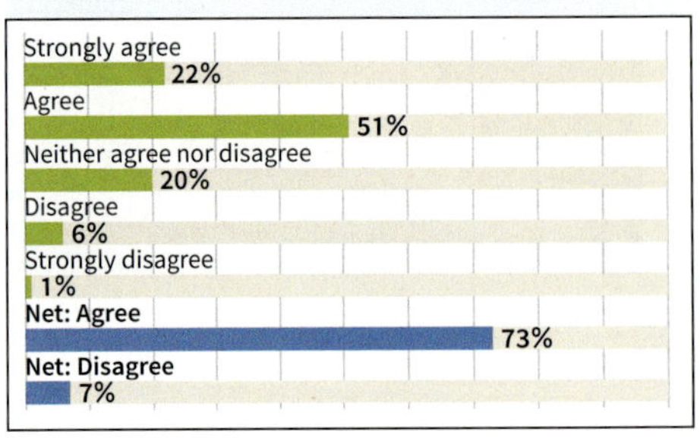

q2. I would be more likely to employ a graduate who had constructive gap year experience involving independent travel, working or volunteering overseas than one who did not.

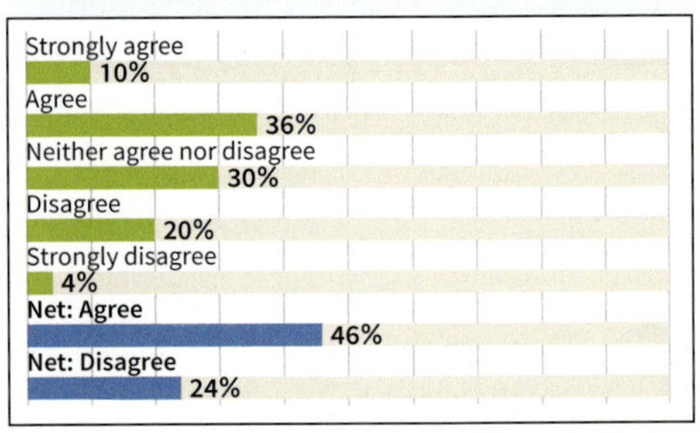

Net: Agree includes those who "agree" and "strongly agree"

q3. For a job-seeker, relevant work experience is more valuable than an average* non-vocational degree*.

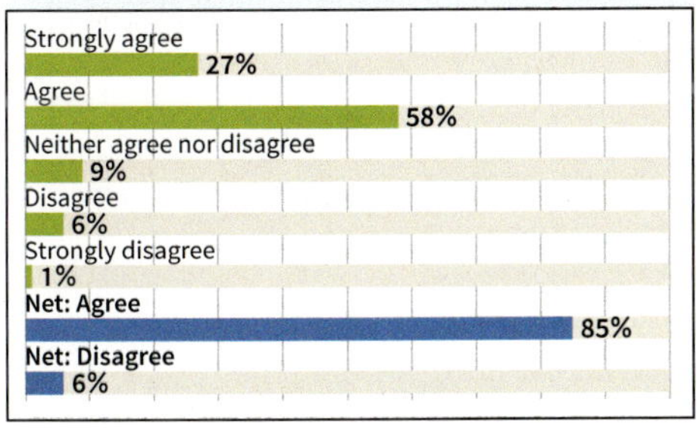

q4. A constructive gap year spent volunteering or gaining work experience overseas makes a job application stand out.

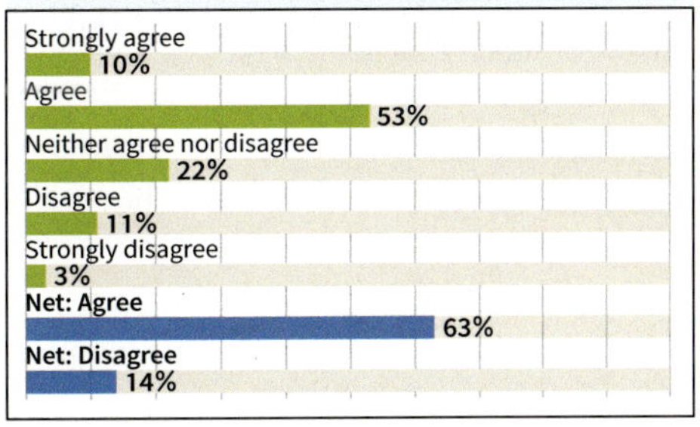

average ordinary
non-vocational degree *nicht berufsbezogene Berufsausbildung*

q5. Young people who take constructive gap years involving independent travel, working or volunteering overseas before going to university tend to get better value from their subsequent* education.

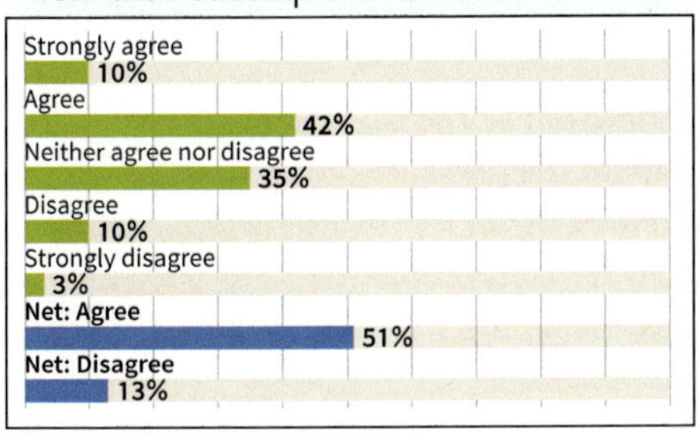

q6. Graduates who have taken gap years involving independent travel, working or volunteering overseas are likely to move up an organisation more swiftly* than those who have not.

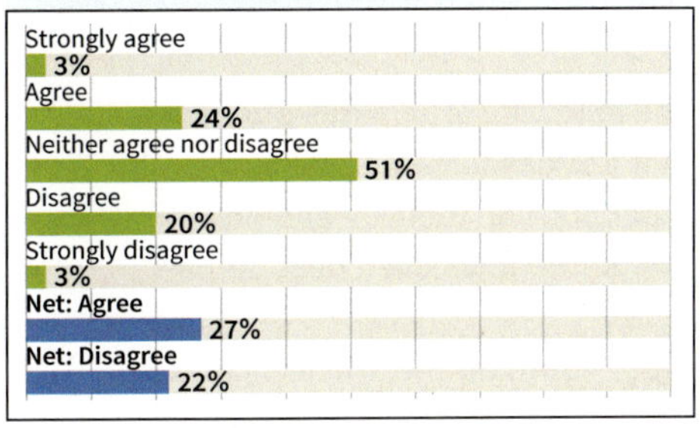

swift fast, quick
subsequent following

q7. Recruits who have taken a gap year involving independent travel, working or volunteering overseas generally appear more settled in their career choice

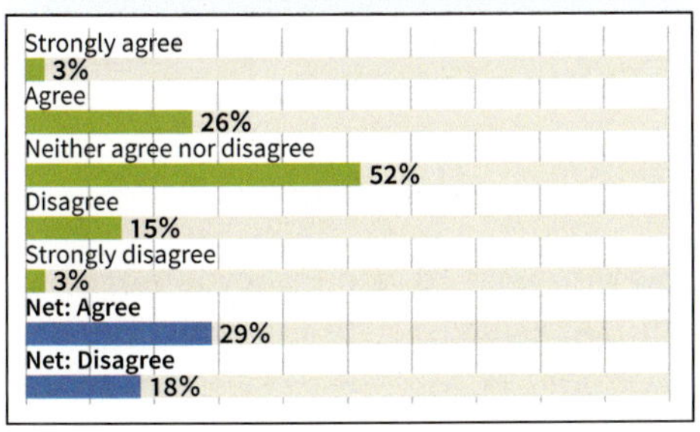

q8. Given a number of equally well-qualified applicants, I would generally favour those with constructive gap year experience over those without.

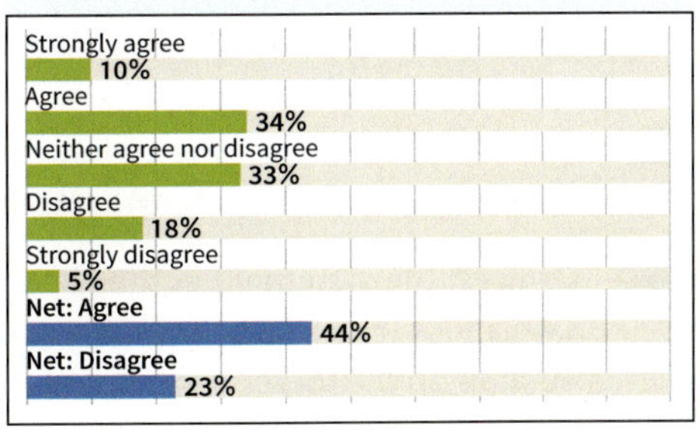

A gap year adds absolutely no value when applying for a job.

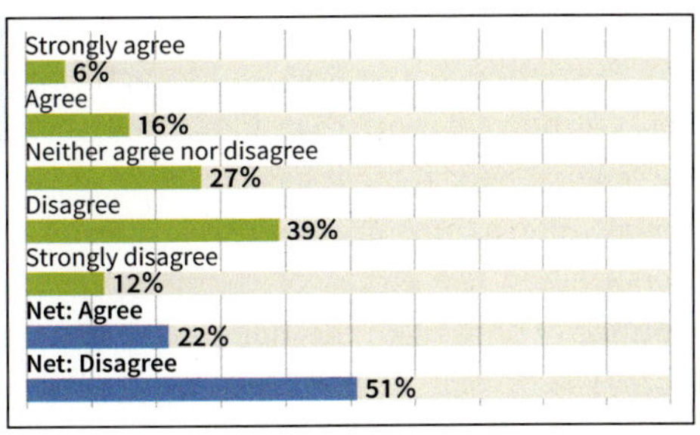

Source: www.yougov.com [04.01.2016]

ZOOM IN: Vocabulary

Talking about figures

- The figures show/illustrate/give information about ...
- The figures can be interpreted as follows...
- A high/low percentage of the Human Resource professionals/the respondents ...
- In comparison, more/fewer Human Resource professionals think that ... would ...
- Over two thirds of ... More than half of ... The overwhelming majority/minority ... Only a few ...
- What is (also) striking is that ...
- From this one can conclude/deduce ... In conclusion ... To sum up, the survey shows ...

M 1b Career-boosting Internships for Sale

Rachel Williams

The following article was published in the British newspaper *The Guardian* on 24 May 2011. In it journalist Rachel Williams informs readers about the pressure on students to get job experience on their CV and how this leads to them working for free in internships, for which they sometimes even need to pay.

1. **Sum up** the article's content.

2. **Explain** the following statements by referring to information given in the article:
   a) "Today, internships are both ubiquitous and highly contentious." (l. 5)
   b) "... asking students to spend large sums for such opportunities harms social mobility ..." (l. 35 f.)
   c) "... employers in the UK are particularly impressed by students who can offer insights into working in China given its importance as a fast-growing economy." (l. 29 ff.)

2. **Examine** the author's line of argument and show how examples and factual information underline the message that is conveyed.

2. **Contrast** the statement in the picture below with what Edward Holroyd Pearce says about the value of unpaid work (l. 31 ff.). Afterwards, state and **justify** your opinion on the topic.

stint period of time
to fumble to handle sth. clumsily
ubiquitous omnipresent
contentious controversial
saddled burdened

humble lowly

About a decade ago the word internships was barely used in a British context. There was work experience, but that was something you did for a couple of weeks while you were at school and was more than likely to involve an unfulfilling stint* fumbling* with the photocopier at a local business. [...]
Today, internships are both ubiquitous* and highly contentious*. There are campaigns denouncing the ethics of requiring young people already saddled* with thousands of pounds of debt from their degree studies to do unpaid work, and debate over the morality of a system that allows those from well-to-do families to exploit their connections and secure opportunities that give them even greater advantage over those from humbler* backgrounds.

Last month, the deputy prime minister, Nick Clegg, called for the trend to be reversed, only for it to turn out that as a teenager he himself had got a placement through his father's influence.

Yet with competition for graduate jobs more intense than ever – last week a survey showed applications were likely to be up by a third this year – internships are still widely accepted as crucial* for those seeking the best positions after university. Demand shows no sign of dropping – and now it seems increasingly that the pressure to bag* a career-boosting placement is leading students not just to work for free, but to pay for the privilege. [...]

crucial very important
to bag to get sth. before others do

Meanwhile firms offering to arrange internships abroad for a fee, usually in China or Australia, are growing in size and number. One, CRCC Asia, has increased the number of placements it offers in Beijing and Shanghai, in areas including law and green technology, fivefold* in three years.

fivefold five times as much

This year, 3,600 students applied for its one or two month internships, easily filling the 1,300 places. It expects to expand further next year and possibly start offering opportunities in Hong Kong. Students, who are assessed for suitability*, pay £1,495 for a month in Bejing and £100 more for Shanghai. As well as a fee for arranging the placement, the figure includes accommodation, a visa and other extras. But students must cover their flights and living costs while in China, separately.

suitability being appropriate

The firm's London director, Edward Holroyd Pearce, says employers in the UK are particularly impressed by students who can offer insights into working in China given its importance as a fast-growing economy. [...] "The fact that students are doing an internship helps them in their applications for a paid job. You need the experience to get the job and if you have to pay for it then it is worth it."

Critics disagree. Already concerned that unpaid internships put poor students at a disadvantage, they say asking students to spend large sums for such opportunities harms social mobility even more.

"It's incredibly worrying that we're moving from a situation where people don't just have to work for free but are having to pay to work," says Ben Lyons, the co-director of *Intern Aware*, which campaigns for interns to be paid the minimum wage. "It puts these experiences and opportunities out of reach of the vast majority of young people." [...]

Martin Birchall, managing director of *High Fliers Research* (HRF), says it's no surprise graduates are so keen to find placements. "Employers have been looking for more than just the basic degree for some time, and the recession* accelerated* that process," he says. "In the past work experience was a 'nice to have'. Now it has, in effect, becoming a prerequisite."

recession period of economic contraction
to accelerate [ək'seləreit] to speed up

The NUS's vice-president for society and citizenship, Susan Nash, is concerned that young people may be having to resort* to funding opportunities abroad. "People shouldn't have to pay to find work experience that enables them to get into the job market," she says. "The government must wake up to the fact that there needs to be more attention to this area."

to resort to to turn to

Paul Redmond, head of careers and employability at Liverpool University, accepts the increased importance of experience, but says: "Students should never have to work for free – and higher education institutions must work to ensure they don't have to. [...]

Rachel Williams, "Career-boosting Internships for Sale", www.theguardian.com, 24.05.2011 [04.01.2016]

M2 The Smart Career Move You Haven't Considered: Working Abroad

Chloe Gray

Despite graduating from college with summa cum laude honours, New Yorker Chloe Gray found herself working in the retail field afterwards. Being very unhappy about her situation, she decided to get a job abroad. She landed an internship with an organisation in Mexico City, which one month later resulted in fulltime employment. She has been living in Mexico for more than three years now and strongly advises young people to consider starting their career abroad.

1. In a Placemat Activity, discuss the benefits of taking on a job abroad. Present your ideas in class.
2. **Outline** the positive aspects of working abroad as presented by Chloe Gray.
3. **Assess** the arguments presented and **discuss** possible negative aspects of moving abroad with a partner.
4. **Comment** on the question whether you would consider working abroad after school or university.

to abide by to act according to
mannerism characteristic manner of doing something
condescending arrogant
to collaborate to work together

agile *here*: mentally aware
compassionate sympathetic

to snag (infml.) to acquire, to secure

You Will Learn to Be Adaptable

Each country abides* by a different set of values, mannerisms*, and customs in the workplace – and when you start working somewhere new, you'll have to adapt fast. For example, Americans tend to value getting to the point in conversations for the sake of efficiency. In Mexico, I quickly learned that being direct with co-workers often comes off as rude and even condescending*, and it won't get you very far if you need to collaborate* with someone. In fact, time spent making a personal connection before talking about business – even if you simply need to ask someone to send you a file – goes a long way here. While it can be frustrating to have to change your working style this drastically, adapting to new conventions teaches you to be more flexible, agile*, and compassionate*. It makes you more sensitive to how other people react to you in a professional setting and makes you an all-around better communicator. When you do move back to your home country, you'll be able to point to this adaptability during interviews – and it will take you far in any job you have.

You Will Have a Better Chance of Taking on High-Level Positions More Quickly

You are most likely well aware that the job market in the U.S., especially in big cities, is highly competitive. On the other hand, if you know the field you want to work in and research which other countries have opportunities in that field, you will likely open yourself up to a much greater chance of snagging* your dream job and taking on more responsibility more quickly in another country.

For example, Mexico and Chile both have cities with interesting tech and start-up scenes – but young folks looking for jobs aren't flocking* to these cities like they are to San Francisco or New York. The relative lack of competition, combined with the fact that many Latin American start-ups like the idea of having a native English speaker with international connections on their team, means that prospects are good for American grads looking for opportunities to grow. The majority of my expat* friends living in Mexico (myself included) were hired into or quickly advanced to high-level positions in their companies – positions that would have taken them many years to work up to in their home countries.

You Will Become Bilingual (As Long As You Don't Only Hang Out With Expats)

There are numerous personal and professional benefits of being bilingual. For one, people who speak more than one language tend to get paid more (as much as 20%!). Also, being bilingual can allow you to form a vital part of a company's growth strategy, whether it is trying to enter new markets on a national level or expand to other countries. Overall, being bilingual is a skill associated with top performers and earners: 31% of executives* speak two languages. And being bilingual is actually proven to make you smarter, as it makes you better at solving complex problems.

This is, of course, assuming you don't only hang out with expats! Enrol in intensive language classes, insist on speaking the native language even when people speak to you in English, and don't give up. I'm pretty bad at languages, and I learned fluent Spanish in nine months – I bet you could do it in six!

You Will Foster a Global Network of Contacts

We've all heard numerous times that the world is becoming increasingly interconnected, and many of us experience this on a daily basis through social media, conference calls with international colleagues, and increased business travel. Working abroad gives you the chance to build relationships with people in your field on an international level, so even when you decide to move back to your home country, you can continue to nurture* these relationships from afar and incorporate them into your new job.

For example, if I were to move back to the U.S., I could position myself as someone who can bring valuable business contacts and high-level knowledge of the region to a company looking to expand into the Latin American market. I could even start a company with a business model based on connecting the Mexican and American markets, using my contacts in both regions as a starting point.

The older we get, the harder it is to drop everything and move to another country, so I strongly advocate* taking a job abroad early in your career so that you can expand your perspective of the world, immerse* yourself in another culture, and gain experiences and skills that will make you stand out against other job candidates. You'll undoubtedly also create some amazing memories along the way.

Chloe Mason Gray, "The Smart Career Move You Haven't Considered: Working Abroad", www.themuse.com [03.01.2016]

to flock to move in huge numbers

expat (expatriate) person who does not live in their own country

executive person in a leading position with supervisory authority in an organisation

to nurture to develop

to advocate to favour, to support
to immerse to involve

M 3a Writing a CV and a Letter of Application

When applying for a job or an internship you will most certainly be required to write a letter of application as well as a CV (BE)/résumé (AE). These documents serve in order to introduce you and your skill set to your future employee. Before writing a letter of application and a CV/résumé you should consider carefully what to include in order to present yourself in the best possible way.

Tel: +49 (0)221 123456

Gartenweg 20
54327 Köln
Germany

your own address in the top right-hand corner

15 May 2016

date of writing

reference number or keywords related to the position

Your ref: TBS/1234

address in full, as on envelope

Roots & Shoots
The Jane Goodall Institute
1595 Spring Hill Road
Vienna, VA 22182
USA

Use "Madam or Sir" if you do not know the name of the person.

Dear Madam or Sir,

introductory paragraph; reason for your letter; start with a capital letter

I am writing to apply for an internship at your institute.
Please find enclosed a copy of my CV.

body of letter; your qualifications; reason(s) why you want the job

Since graduating from St. Thomas Grammar School, I have gained experience in working with various environmental groups as well as in a zoo. I have also had the opportunity of working in an animal shelter and have experienced the importance of giving more to these animals than just medical treatment.

I would welcome the opportunity to work in one of your camps and look forward to your response.

Yours faithfully

If you started with "Dear Madam or Sir," end with "Yours faithfully". If you know the surname, e. g. "Dear Ms. Brown," end with "Yours sincerely".

Sign your name and print it in full afterwards.

T. Müller
Tobias Müller
Enc. CV

Curriculum Vitae

Name	Tobias Müller
Address	Gartenweg 20 54327 Köln (Cologne)
Telephone No.	+49(0)221 123456
Mobile	+49(0)1723456789
Email	tobymueller@web.de
Nationality	German
Date/place of birth	25 July 1999, Cologne
Profile	a highly motivated and creative Graduate from a Grammar School with experience in animal care
Education	
2009 – 2017	Grammar School (A-Level)
2005 – 2009	Elementary School
Employment/	practical work as animal caretaker/ keeper in a zoo and at an animal shelter
Interests	judo, tennis, music

- only refer to your most relevant qualifications or skills
- if possible, you can include references (= people that can be contacted in order to give a judgement of your qualifications, experience, character, etc.)
- enclose photocopies of relevant certificates
- begin with the most recent employment/qualification and work backwards

Zoom in: Vocabulary

I noted with interest ... ■ I am writing in response to ... ■ With reference to your advertisement in ... ■ As you can see from my CV, ... ■ I am currently studying at ... ■ Having gained a degree in ..., ■ This position interests me because ... ■ I would be grateful for the opportunity to ... ■ I have extensive experience in ... ■ I am available for an interview ... ■ If you consider my qualifications to be suitable ...

Iris Edelbrock (Hg.), Pathway Advanced. Lese- und Arbeitsbuch für die Qualifikationsphase der gymnasialen Oberstufe, Schöningh, Paderborn 2015, p. 535

M 3b Blind Applying

Blind Applying is an internship program initiated by *Deutsche Telekom* and powered by Entrypark, Nyggränd 10, 11130 Stockholm, in Sweden. Many notable companies such as *Daimler* or *ThyssenKrupp* make use of the program. As implied in the name of the program, participants apply blindly with just one CV/résumé for a large number of internships, with no idea where they might be employed if their application proves to be successful. The project takes place annually with an application period stretching from October to December. The internships begin in the summer of the following year. Every enrolled student is invited to apply no matter what and where he/she studies, but the application has to be written in the English language. All applications are free of charge.

1. Against the backdrop of what you know about *Blind Applying*, discuss the meaning of the following statement that is presented in *Blind Applying's* advertisement video on YouTube: "Success is not always a straight line".

2. Get familiar with the requirements of *Blind Applying* by visiting their website www.blindapplying.com and brainstorm with a partner what an application would need in order to stand out.

3. Write a blind application (letter of application and CV/résumé) in response to the programme. Before you start writing your application, think thoroughly about the qualifications and skills you have to offer. Use the shell model overleaf for help.

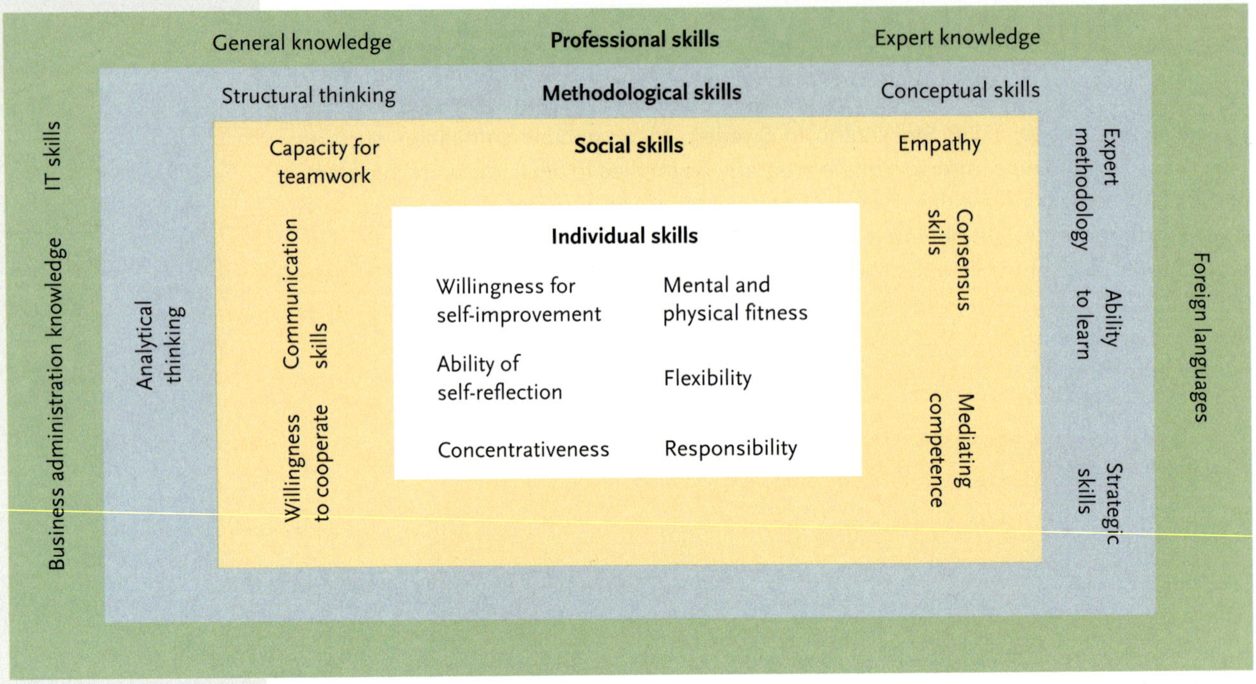

Iris Edelbrock (Hg.), Pathway Advanced. Lese- und Arbeitsbuch für die Qualifikationsphase der gymnasialen Oberstufe, Schöningh, Paderborn 2015, p. 483

M 3c Conducting a Job Interview

If your application is successful you will be asked to come in for a job interview in which the company wants to find out if your personality matches its requirements. Most likely you will be asked questions about your personal history, your career goals and your work habits.

1. Familiarise yourself with the questions below and together with a partner choose one question from each category that you think is most relevant. Discuss how you would answer them.

Zoom in: Tip

Possible job interview questions for employers

Questions about yourself

- What is your greatest strength?
- What is your greatest weakness?
- What motivates you?
- How do you evaluate success?
- How would you describe yourself?
- How would a friend/a colleague describe you?
- ...

Behavioural questions
- Tell me about how you worked effectively under pressure.
- Are you a risk taker?
- How do you cope with failure?
- ...

Questions concerning your career goals
- What are your goals for the next five/ten years?
- How do you plan to achieve those goals?
- Describe your dream job.
- Describe the perfect working atmosphere.
- ...

About co-workers
- Tell me about a time that you participated in a team – what was your role?
- Do you prefer to work independently or in a team?
- How do you deal with criticism from co-workers?
- ...

Questions related to the company
- Why do you want this job?
- Why do you wish to work for this company?
- Why should we employ you?
- ...

Iris Edelbrock (Hg.), Pathway Advanced. Lese- und Arbeitsbuch für die Qualifikationsphase der gymnasialen Oberstufe, Schöningh, Paderborn 2015, Zusatzmaterial

Zoom in: Tip

Before being interviewed you should research the company and obtain an overview:
- What is the full and correct name of the company?
- When and by whom was the company founded?
- What are the most important facts regarding the company's history?
- Where are the headquarters/branches situated?
- Who leads the company (CEO – Chief Executive Officer)?
- How is the company organised/structured?
- Which products/services are most successful?
- What are the company's plans for the future?

2. Get together in groups of three and perform a role play in which you conduct a job interview. One of you will be the observer who takes notes on the interview and provides feedback afterwards, the other two will be the interviewer and the interviewee. Make use of the role cards provided.
After having conducted the interview talk about the performance (feedback).
- How did you feel?
- What was good? What can be improved?
- What would you do differently next time?
- ...

When you are finished, switch roles.

Role A – Interviewer

Your name is John/Jane Doe and you work for the National Archives and Records Administration in Washington D.C. The NARA is an independent agency of the United States government charged with preserving and documenting government and historical records and with increasing public access to these documents, which, in effect, comprise the National Archives.
Your department plans to organise an exhibition about American-German relations throughout history. Therefore, you need a qualified German citizen interested in the history of the US and Germany, who is also able to speak English fluently.

In your interview with ... from Germany, you should ask questions from the box provided. In addition, you should refer to the following points:

- beginning: greet the applicant and introduce yourself
- internship is based in Washington D.C. → applicant's readiness to live in Washington
- applicant's experience with the American culture
- applicant's reasons for wanting to do the internship
- applicant's interest in American and German history
- applicant's former work experience
- applicant's ability to speak English
- applicant's computer literacy
- offer of paying travel expenses and providing accommodation
- end: finish the conversation and say he/she will hear from you within the next week

Role B – Interviewee

You have applied for an internship with the National Archives and Records Administration in Washington D.C. The NARA is an independent agency of the United States government charged with preserving and documenting government and historical records and with increasing public access to those documents, which, in effect, comprise the National Archives.
One of their departments plans to organise an exhibition about US-German relations throughout history, which is why they need a German citizen interested in the history of the US and Germany who is also able to speak English fluently.

In your interview with John/Jane Doe from the National Archives and Records Administration in Washington D.C. you will be asked questions from the box provided. Prepare to answer them in an appropriate way. Furthermore, you should refer to the following points:

- beginning: greet the interviewer and introduce yourself
- state your motivation for the internship
- talk about your stays in foreign countries
- refer to any skills you have that might be helpful for the job
- talk about your personal interest in history, especially American-German relations
- emphasize any proof of your ability to speak English (certificates or bilingual education?)
- refer to work experience or other internships
- ask for help concerning your accommodation
- ask about the planned salary
- end: emphasize your interest in the project and your willingness to participate

Role C – Observer

The following role play is an interview between a staff manager of the National Archives and Records Administration in Washington D.C. and an applicant for an internship. The NARA is an independent agency of the United States government charged with preserving and documenting government and historical records and with increasing public access to those documents, which, in effect, comprise the National Archives.

Your job is to observe the interviewee carefully in order to give him/her feedback on his/her performance. Your feedback will be very important for the interviewee in helping him/her to improve. Make sure you note down both the weaknesses and the strengths of the interviewee during the role play. Pay special attention to the following aspects:

- appearance (dress, body language, eye contact)
- usage of appropriate language (formal register)
- ability to answer questions appropriately
- ability to emphasize suitability for and interest in the job
- realistic self-assessment
- (knowledge about company/organisation)

- Which characteristics did the applicant display during the interview? To what extent was he/she ...

□ confident	□ achievement-oriented
□ cooperative	□ responsible
□ outgoing	□ open
□ dedicated	□ mature
□ professional	□ convincing

➔ Can you give examples justifying your assessment?

M 4a Modern Globalisation Increasingly Changing the Labour Market

Walesbiz

The following text was blogged by the user Walesbiz and was published on a Welsh business blog. The author comments on the impact of modern globalisation on the labour market and on the effects of the replacement of Generation X with Generation Y.

1. Have a look at the pictures below and make an educated guess about their association with the changing labour market.
2. **Present** the numbers and data related to the changing labour market.
3. **Explain** the impact of the changing generations.
4. **Assess** the importance of the changing labour market for your own career.

Zoom in: Terminology

Generation X

Generation X (Gen X) is the generation born after the post-World War II baby boom. Generation X was born between the early 1960s and the early 1980s.

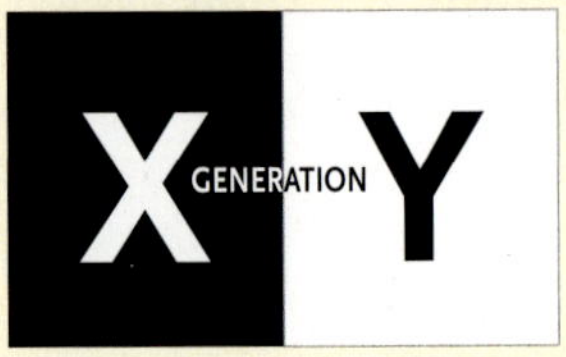

Generation Y

Generation Y are the demographic cohort following Generation X. They are also known as the *Millennial Generation* or *Millennials.* Generation Y was born between the early 1980s and the early 2000s.

Person using the internet

The Fall of the Berlin Wall in 1989

The increasing GDP (Gross Domestic Product) of China and India

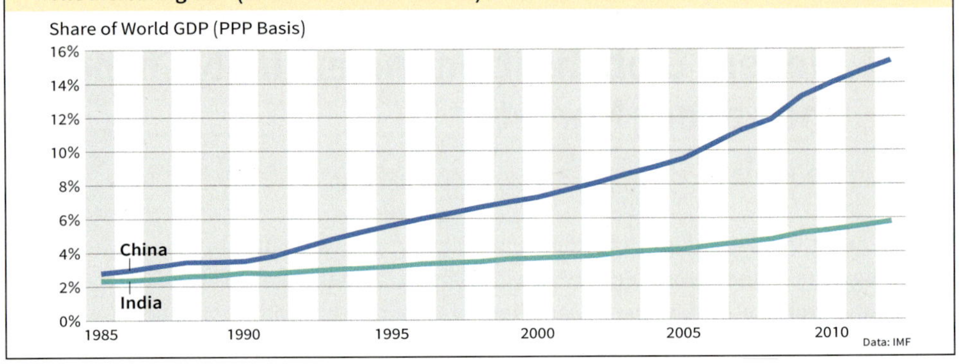

Modern globalisation is having a huge impact on the labour market through a new generation of workers willing to be internationally mobile.
Willingness – or, in many cases, desire – to work abroad is becoming a key trend.
Globalisation requires us to move faster to keep up with the competition. The fall of the Berlin wall, the growing influence of the Internet and the rise of China and India, mean that the global labour market is also becoming competitive.

Three major trends now characterise the future of the global labour market. These are: a willingness to be internationally mobile, the globalisation of labour markets and the impact of 'Generation Y'.

Recruitment research has noted an increase in the amount of people willing to be mobile in the international labour market, indicating people are keener* to move around. Willingness to work abroad depends on whether people want to live and work in a new environment and whether they are tired of their home country. Working abroad can also be driven by the need to get closer to relatives or learn a new language or culture.

keen enthusiastic

Another reason for working overseas is the economic situation at home. This isn't the actual state of the economy of the home country, but its perceived* state. This perception can be a result of a short-term financial crisis or a slow rate of growth, as we've seen in the UK construction sector.

perceived believed

Then we have a major trend in the globalisation of labour markets. In 2006 barely anybody used search engines like Google for job-hunting. By 2009 this method was used by over 40 percent of job seekers.

When looking for jobs in local markets, 41 percent of respondents in the Global Talent Mobility Research study said they would use search engines. When job-hunting internationally, this number rose to 49 percent.

Besides the use of search engines, important developments have emerged* with job boards*, affecting the effectiveness of international job-hunting. As in the case of search engines, this made it easier to search for jobs in the global labour market.

to emerge to become known
job board online service to advertise jobs

Three types of job boards can be identified:

- Local job boards exist to search for jobs within a home country, and within a local labour market.
- Job boards abroad are job boards for a variety of markets in specific countries, however many of these job boards aren't user friendly.
- International job boards combine local job boards into one search and allow a job-hunter to search for similar jobs across multiple countries simultaneously.

People looking for a job abroad make even greater use of social media – 35 percent of respondents in the Global Talent Mobility Research said they would use social media when searching for jobs. Just three years ago, this wasn't the case: respondents to the 2006 study didn't mention social media at all.

Then we have ageing workforces due to the baby-boom generation. These workers will soon retire. The next generation, Generation Y, is anybody born between 1980 and the early 1990s.

Gen Y will form a bigger part of the active workforce in the coming years, affecting attitudes towards employment in general. The entry of Gen Y into the workforce and the simultaneous decline of the baby-boomers will have a notable impact on the global labour market.

Three characteristics for Gen Y are: They were raised using computers and other digital devices, resulting in a greater use of digital job-hunting methods; they are more predisposed* to studying abroad, resulting in students leaving their home country; and it's common for them to go backpacking after finishing college or university, aided by today's cheaper flights.

predisposed inclined, willing

Gen Y are therefore more international and more outward looking than their predecessors*, impacting* levels of international labour mobility.

predecessors *Vorgänger*
to impact to influence

Research shows that the younger somebody is, the more willing he or she is to be mobile in the global labour market. The desire to explore different cultures, the opportunity to meet new people, to link up with overseas family, or simply a better climate are more important reasons for this age group. [...]

Walesbiz, "Modern Globalisation Increasingly Changing the Labour Market", www.walesbusiness.org, 28.07.2014 [03.01.2016]

M 4b Wie die Flüchtlingskrise den Arbeitsmarkt verändert

Simone Jansen

Not all effects of the ongoing migration crisis are negative. In the following column written for the German business news magazine *Wirtschaftswoche*, Simone Jansen highlights creative ideas concerning the integration of refugees into the job market. In doing so, she also draws attention to jobs created by the refugees themselves or jobs that arise as a direct result of the refugee crisis.

1. As illustrated in **M 4a**, historical and current events effectively shape the labour market. Currently, the ongoing migration crisis has a significant impact on the European job market. Make an educated guess how the crisis might influence the job market in a negative as well as in a positive way. Arrange these aspects in column form.

2. You have been asked by your British exchange partner to contribute to his school's magazine. As the negative reactions towards the refugee crisis are omnipresent in both your countries, he wants you to write about positive reactions in Germany. For this purpose **present** the relevant information given in the article below.

Refugees in front of a German employment agency

Die Reaktionen auf die aktuelle Flüchtlingswelle, die uns in den Medien vermittelt werden, schwanken zwischen Hilfsbereitschaft und Willkommenskultur sowie Skepsis und Angst vor der immensen Aufgabe. Dabei gibt es längst eine dritte Sichtweise im Umgang mit dem an sich schwierigen Thema: eine pragmatische, die hilft, kreative Lösungen für Probleme zu finden. Ein Umdenken*, das innovative Ideen hervorbringt, aus denen auch mehr werden kann, als ein spontanes Projekt.

Zudem entstehen rund um das Thema Flüchtlinge tausende neue Jobs. Denn Not macht bekanntlich erfinderisch, auch wenn es abgedroschen* klingt. Und mal ehrlich: Haben wir eigentlich eine andere Wahl?

Umdenken rethinking

abgedroschen hackneyed, banal, corny

Eines der vordringlichsten Probleme wird die Integration der Flüchtlinge auf dem Arbeitsmarkt sein. Seit dem 6. beziehungsweise 11. November 2014 gelten laut GGUA* Flüchtlingshilfe e. V. für Asylsuchende mit Aufenthaltserlaubnis und Personen mit Duldung folgende Regelung: Die Wartefrist für die Arbeitserlaubnis verkürzt sich von bisher neun beziehungsweise zwölf Monaten auf die ersten drei Monate des Aufenthalts. Danach ist ein nachrangiger Arbeitsmarktzugang möglich.

Hierbei muss für eine konkrete Beschäftigung eine Erlaubnis bei der Ausländerbehörde beantragt werden, die wiederum die Zustimmung der Zentralstelle für Arbeitsvermittlung (ZAV) benötigt. Ohne die Zustimmung des ZAV können Flüchtlinge Ausbildungen und Praktika beginnen oder Jobs für Hochqualifizierte antreten, sofern sie mehr als 47.600 Euro brutto im Jahr verdienen. Erst nach vier Jahren können alle Jobs angenommen werden. Eine Zustimmung der Ausländerbehörde ist aber dennoch in allen Fällen nötig.

Das könnte sich ändern, denn nicht nur Daimler-Chef Dieter Zetsche will gezielt Flüchtlinge als Arbeitskräfte gewinnen und prognostiziert ein neues Wirtschaftswunder; auch Sterne-Koch Heinz Winkler bildet Flüchtlinge aus und die Bundesagentur für Arbeit richtet in Flüchtlingslagern Integration Points ein. Daneben entstehen durch die Flüchtlinge auch neue Jobs: Laut „Bild"-Zeitung benötigt Deutschland jetzt 20000 bis 25000 neue Lehrer, 20000 Mitarbeiter im öffentlichen Dienst, 15000 Polizisten, 50000 Sozialarbeiter und 6000 Ärzte.

Mediales Aufsehen erregten David Jacob und Philipp Kühn. Die beiden Studierenden des Kommunikationsdesigns haben als Bachelorarbeit die Seite Workeer.de gebaut, eine Jobbörse, die speziell Flüchtlinge mit potentiellen Arbeitgebern zusammenbringen soll. 868 Bewerber, 1508 Jobs und 1102 Arbeitgeber präsentieren sich bislang hier mit Profilen, Fotos, Angaben zu Sprachkenntnissen usw. Einen Schritt weiter geht das Projekt refupreneur.eu, das aus Flüchtlingen Unternehmer* machen will und Flüchtlinge beim Crowdfunding unterstützen will.

Da eines der Grundprobleme bei der Jobsuche die deutsche Sprache darstellt, will das Projekt „German for Refugees" Flüchtlinge sowie potentielle Arbeitgeber mit einer Deutschkurs-Suchmaschine unterstützen.

Ende Oktober findet in Berlin der „Refugee-Hackathon"* statt, bei dem digitale Lösungen für Probleme wie die Abstimmung von Spenden oder bürokratische* Hindernisse bei der Integration gefunden werden sollen. [...]

Auch die deutsche Personal-Blogger-Szene hat das Thema Flüchtlinge für sich entdeckt: Thomas Eggert, Geschäftsführer der BEGIS GmbH*, rief kürzlich die Personaler auf, etwas Historisches zu tun und hat eine so genannte Blogparade zum Thema HR* und Flüchtlinge gestartet. Sebastian Wolking rollt auf Karrierebibel.de das Thema von der anderen Seite auf: Er listet auf, welche Jobs durch die Flüchtlingswelle entstehen oder vermehrt zu besetzen sind, etwa beim Bundesamt für Migration und Flüchtlinge: Das sind vor allem Sachbearbeiter, Dolmetscher, Wissenschaftliche Mitarbeiter für empirische Sozialforschung, Informatiker und Bürokaufleute.

6000 neue Stellen wollen Bund und Länder* rund um die Flüchtlinge schaffen, der Personalmarketing-Experte Henner Knabenreich nennt in seinem Blog die Details: „Nordrhein-Westfalen will alleine in diesem Jahr 792 neue Arbeitsplätze ausschreiben – davon 674 als ‚Flüchtlingskinderunterrichter'. Bayern sucht ‚Flüchtlingsheimbewacher' bzw. ‚Lagerordner'. Hessen stellt im nächsten Jahr 190 Personen ein, vor allem als ‚Erstaufnahmeeinrichtungsentlaster'. Oder als ‚Flüchtlingsregistrierer'." [...]

Simone Janson, „Wie die Flüchtlingskrise den Arbeitsmarkt verändert", www.wiwo.de, 14.10.2015 [03.01.2016]

GGUA Gemeinnützige Gesellschaft zur Unterstützung Asylsuchender e. V.

Unternehmer entrepreneur

Refugee-Hackathon 24 to 25 October 2015
bürokratisch bureaucratic [ˌbjʊərəˈkrætɪk]

BEGIS GmbH Beratungsgesellschaft für Informationssysteme
HR Human Resources, Personalwesen

Bund und Länder federal government and federal states

M 5 Why Are White People Expats When the Rest of Us Are Immigrants?

Mawuna Remarque Koutonin

Mawuna Remarque Koutonin is the editor of "Silicon.Africa", a blog which comments on African issues and offers an opinion on how to change existing structures. He describes himself as a freedom fighter and African cause activist. The following article was published by *The Guardian*.

1. Take a look at the photo and guess which travelling person is an immigrant or an expatriate. Where is the difference?
2. In your own words, **present** the different use of the terms 'expat' and 'immigrant'.
3. **Analyse** the stylistic devices in the article.
4. **Comment** on the problems of the use of different terms for 'global' workers when working in an international team.

lexicon word pool, vocabulary

In the lexicon* of human migration there are still hierarchical words, created with the purpose of putting white people above everyone else. One of those remnants is the word "expat".

What is an expat? And who is an expat? According to Wikipedia, "an expatriate (often shortened to expat) is a person temporarily or permanently residing in a country other than that of the person's upbringing. The word comes from the Latin terms ex ('out of') and patria ('country, fatherland')".

Defined that way, you should expect that any person going to work outside of his or her country for a period of time would be an expat, regardless of his skin colour or country. But that is not the case in reality; expat is a term reserved exclusively for western white people going to work abroad.

Africans are immigrants. Arabs are immigrants. Asians are immigrants. However, Europeans are expats because they can't be at the same level as other ethnicities. They are superior. Immigrants is a term set aside for "inferior* races".

inferior *here*: lower

Don't take my word for it. The Wall Street Journal, the leading financial information magazine in the world, has a blog dedicated to the life of expats and recently they featured a story "Who is an expat, anyway?". Here are the main conclusions: "Some arrivals are described as expats; others as immigrants; and some simply as migrants. It depends on social class, country of origin and economic status. It's strange to hear some people in Hong Kong described as expats, but not others. Anyone with roots in a western country is considered an expat ... Filipino domestic helpers are just guests, even if they've been here for decades. Mandarin-speaking mainland Chinese are rarely regarded as expats ... It's a double standard woven into official policy."

The reality is the same in Africa and Europe. Top African professionals going to work in Europe are not considered expats. They are immigrants. Period. "I work for multinational organisations both in the private and public sectors. And being black or coloured doesn't gain me the term 'expat'. I'm a highly qualified immigrant, as they call me, to be politically correct," says an African migrant worker.

Most white people deny that they enjoy the privileges of a racist system. And why not? But our responsibility is to point out and to deny them these privileges, directly related to an outdated supremacist ideology. If you see those "expats" in Africa, call them immigrants like everyone else. If that hurts their white superiority*, they can jump in the air and stay there. The political deconstruction* of this outdated worldview must continue.

superiority dominance

deconstruction dismantling, removal

Mawuna Remarque Koutonin, "Why Are White People Expats When the Rest of Us Are Immigrants?", www.theguardian.com, 27.04.2015 [24.09.2015] Copyright Guardian New & Media Ltd 2016

M 6 Letter to an Expat

Sara Elhassan

Sara Elhassan is a freelance writer and editor who is based in Khartoum, Sudan. She publishes her critical thoughts on social, political as well as personal issues on her blog "alucan.wordpress.com". One of her poems, which she wrote in reaction to statements made by a Sudanese professor, received a lot of attention in the social media.

1. Pick three terms from the word cloud and **explain** in how far the terms are related.

2. The term 'expatriate' usually refers to western people living for short-term or long-term assignments in a foreign country. Can you think of problems which may arise in the encounter between expats and local people?

3. **Point out** the experiences which led the author to write this letter.

4. **Analyse** the tone of the text.

5. **Justify** this letter to an expat and its demand for refraining from using the word 'expat'.

Dear expat (immigrant) living in Sudan,

Kindly refrain* from speaking about Sudan if you've only been to one place in it (Khartoum). Kindly refrain from giving us your opinion on the country if you know virtually 'nothing' about it. Kindly refrain from speaking on Sudanese life and issues if you have no Sudanese friends while living in Sudan. Particularly, kindly refrain from speaking on Sudanese life and issues if you are uninterested/afraid/repulsed* by the idea of making Sudanese friends or getting to know Sudanese people.

On a similar note, kindly refrain from referring to Sudanese people as "the locals". Kindly refrain from pointing out how (lit.) poor Sudanese folk are "probably so much happier" than you and your expat friends, because they have 'heart' or 'soul' or whatever word you use to infantilize* people. And while you're at it, kindly refrain from sharing your "surprise" whenever you meet a Sudanese person who is fluent in your mother tongue, particularly if it's English. English is not special, so kindly refrain the next time you feel the urge* to ask, "Where did you learn English?" or "But, you don't even have an accent!".

Kindly refrain from portraying yourself as "roughing it in Africa" if you live on a compound*. Kindly refrain from portraying yourself as "roughing it in Africa" if your job gives you housing, a car, and monthly stipend* beyond your salary. Kindly refrain from portraying yourself as "roughing it in Africa" if you only frequent places where the majority of other patrons are expats like yourself [...]. OH, and KINDLY refrain from complimenting something by saying "I felt like I wasn't even in Sudan!" – especially to a Sudanese person's face.

This one will probably be the most difficult, because as a people we have the tendency and urge to please, but kindly refrain from disappointment the next time a Sudanese person is not 'overly' kind to you, or doesn't care that you're present in the room. Kindly refrain from being indignant* when you aren't given special treatment, or the next time a Sudanese person disagrees with you on something. Kindly refrain from calling them 'rude' because they had a difference of opinion.

Lastly, kindly refrain from offense when someone calls you an immigrant. Kindly refrain from correcting them "actually, it's expat". Semantics aside, immigrant is not an insult. It is not a cuss word*. It is not a slur* or derogatory* label. It is a word that means you moved from your country to live in another. Your offense highlights the negative connotation you've put on it, and thus your own prejudice.

So kindly, refrain.

Sara Elhassan: "Dear Expat", http://alucan.wordpress.com, 28.07.2015 [30.12.2015]

to refrain from sth./from doing sth. to stop doing sth.

repulsed to show strong dislike/disgust

to infantilize sb. to treat sb. as though they are a child

urge need/desire

compound an area surrounded by a fence or wall in which a group of buildings is standing

stipend *Bezüge* (employers of international companies sometimes get a higher salary during their time of working abroad)

indignant at/about sth. feeling/showing anger and surprise because you feel treated unfairly

cuss word swear word

slur insult

derogatory insulting

M7 Cultural Intelligence

P. Christopher Earley, Elaine Mosakowski

Dr. P. Christopher Earley is a professor for Business Economy and Dean of the Tasmanian School of Business and Economics. His research interests include cultural aspects of global business and of globally acting companies. His academic career took him to numerous universities all over the world, among them the London Business School. Elaine Mosakowski is a professor of Management. Currently, she holds a post as professor at Purdue University Krannert School of Management. The following essay was published in the *Harvard Business Review*.

1. **Describe** the cartoon and **explain** the cultural misunderstandings.
2. Take an educated guess about what the concept of 'cultural intelligence' may refer to. Give examples for your explanation.
3. **Outline** the term 'cultural intelligence' on the basis of the text.
4. **Explain** the cultural conflict between the American manager and the German engineers (ll. 19–25).
5. **Discuss** whether 'cultural training' should be part of the training schedule of any medium-sized to big company. Also consider the question of who needs to adapt to the other culture's customs.

[...] Culture is so powerful it can affect how even a lowly insect is perceived*. So it should come as no surprise that the human actions, gestures, and speech patterns a person encounters* in a foreign business setting are subject to an even wider range of interpretations, including ones that can make misunderstandings likely and cooperation impossible. But occasionally an outsider has a seemingly natural ability to interpret someone's

to perceive sb./sth. to see sb./sth.

to encounter to meet

ambiguous unclear, having different meanings
compatriots people of the same country
aptitude: *Begabung*
borrower *Kreditnehmer*

to grasp to understand

to tease out of *etw. herauskitzeln*

idiosyncratic [ˌɪdiəˈsɪŋˈkrætɪk] specific

to float an idea to suggest/put forward an idea
to condemn sth/sb to express disapproval
stunted inadequate, backward
immature childish
modicum *Mindestmaß*
merit value
to modulate to adapt
candor *Offenheit*

to devise to develop
alien foreign, different
coherence consistency

to disarm here: to make sb. feel less angry
demeanor [dɪˈmiːnər] behaviour
to mirror to reflect
esteem *wertschätzen*

efficacy [ˈefikəsi] *Wirkungskraft*
to persevere [pəːsiˈviə] *durchhalten*

unfamiliar and ambiguous* gestures in just the way that person's compatriots* and colleagues would, even to mirror them. We call that *cultural intelligence* or *CQ*. In a world where crossing boundaries is routine, CQ becomes a vitally important aptitude* and skill, and not just for international bankers and borrowers*.

Cultural intelligence: an outsider's seemingly natural ability to interpret someone's unfamiliar and ambiguous gestures the way that person's compatriots would. [...]

Cultural intelligence is related to emotional intelligence, but it picks up where emotional intelligence leaves off. A person with high emotional intelligence grasps* what makes us human and at the same time what makes each of us different from one another. A person with high cultural intelligence can somehow tease* out of a person's or group's behavior those features that would be true of all people and all groups, those peculiar to this person or this group, and those that are neither universal nor idiosyncratic*. The vast realm that lies between those two poles is culture.

An American expatriate manager we know had his cultural intelligence tested while serving on a design team that included two German engineers. As other team members floated* their ideas, the engineers condemned* them repeatedly as stunted* or immature* or worse. The manager concluded that Germans in general are rude and aggressive. A modicum* of cultural intelligence would have helped the American realize he was mistakenly equating the merit* of an idea with the merit of the person presenting it and that the Germans were able to make a sharp distinction between the two. [...]

An expatriate manager who was merely emotionally intelligent would probably have empathized with the team members whose ideas were being criticized, modulated* his or her spontaneous reaction to the engineers' conduct, and proposed a new style of discussion that preserved candor* but spared feelings, if indeed anyone's feelings had been hurt. But without being able to tell how much of the engineers' behavior was idiosyncratic and how much was culturally determined, he or she would not have known how to influence their actions or how easy it would be to do that. [...]

The Three Sources of Cultural Intelligence [...]

Head.

[...] [A] newcomer needs to devise* what we call learning strategies. Although most people find it difficult to discover a point of entry into alien* cultures, whose very coherence* can make them seem like separate, parallel worlds, an individual with high cognitive CQ notices clues to a culture's shared understandings. [...]

Body.

You will not disarm* your foreign hosts, guests, or colleagues simply by showing you understand their culture; your actions and demeanor* must prove that you have already to some extent entered their world. Whether it's the way you shake hands or order a coffee, evidence of an ability to mirror* the customs and gestures of the people around you will prove that you esteem* them well enough to want to be like them. By adopting people's habits [...], you eventually come to understand in the most elemental way what it is like to be them. [...]

Heart.

Adapting to a new culture involves overcoming obstacles and setbacks. People can do that only if they believe in their own efficacy*. If they persevered* in the face of challenging situations in the past, their confidence grew. Confidence is always rooted in mastery of a particular task or set of circumstances. [...]

Elaine Mosakowski, P. Christopher Earley, "Cultural Intelligence", https://hbr.org, October 2004 [24.09.2015]

M 8 Business Etiquette: The Importance of Cultural Sensitivity

Jenny Hirschkorn

The following article was published in the British newspaper *The Telegraph* on 30 January 2014 and deals with the importance of displaying sensitivity in connection with unfamiliar cultural customs.

1. Look at the photo below which depicts South Korean President Park Geun-hye and Bill Gates shaking hands. Speculate why this picture caused international uproar.
2. **Sum up** the content of the article.
3. **Explain** what Neil Payne means when he states that it is important to "do your homework" before venturing to a new territory (ll. 28/29).
4. Follow Payne's advice and "do your homework" by making inquiries about a country of your choice in which you would like to work. Inform your classmates about the country's basic social customs and other culture-related peculiarities that they should be aware of.

Patterned leggings might seem an innocuous* enough product, but when Nike launched its new range in the New Zealand market last summer it was in for a shock.

The designs were inspired by the traditional tattoos of Fiji, Samoa and New Zealand, but the sportswear manufacturer soon faced a petition objecting to the product, on the ground they were a violation of the indigenous people of the Pacific. After about 750 people signed the petition, Nike withdrew* the leggings.

This was a clear demonstration of the importance of cultural sensitivities, even when dealing with English-speaking countries.

Nowhere is this more apparent than between the UK and the United States, frequently described as two nations divided by a common language. That has most certainly been the experience of Martin Brooks, production and export manager of pet nutrition* company Hilton Herbs.

Although the company exports to 42 countries, Mr Brooks considers the US one of the most challenging. "As an example, we had a product for older horses and dogs called Veteran," he says.

innocuous [iˈnɒkjuəs] harmless

to withdraw to take back

nutrition food

connotation implication, undertone

chasm ['kæzəm] abyss, a deep opening

case in point example

to venture to dare to go

crucial very important

paved covered
pitfalls possible dangers

"It didn't really sell in America. Then, a couple of years ago, we were exhibiting at a show there and somebody came across and said that the word had connotations* of war rather than older animals. We changed the name to Senior and now sales have really taken off."

If such a large cultural divide can exist between two countries that share a common mother tongue, how much wider must the chasm* be between nations that speak different languages.

Japan is a case in point* and another very important market for Hilton Herbs, but Mr Brooks says that the way business is done there is very different from the Western model. "We have a much more personal relationship with our distributor there," he says. "A lot of time is spent talking about family and issues not directly connected to the business, but that's every bit as important as nailing down the final order."

At Kwintessential, which specialises in translation and cross-cultural awareness training, founder and marketing director Neil Payne stresses the importance of doing your homework before venturing* into a new territory. Working with colleagues or clients from different cultures can be a minefield, he warns.

"Whether it's localising your website or sending people to conduct business abroad, being aware of things such as cultural, religious, moral, behavioural and linguistic differences is crucial*," he says.

He acknowledges that it is rarely practical to gain an in-depth knowledge of the local language, but just by learning a few basic phrases you show respect and that you are taking the relationship seriously.

There is, of course, another type of language that is every bit as important as the spoken or written word when it comes to effective communication: body language. Bill Gates recently landed in hot water when he shook hands with President Park Geun-hye of South Korea while keeping his left hand in his pocket – a sign of disrespect in that part of the world.

The road to export success is paved* with such pitfalls* and taking the time to learn how to avoid them could prove a very valuable investment.

Jenny Hirschkorn, "Business etiquette: the importance of cultural sensitivity", www.telegraph.co.uk, 30.01.2014 [03.01.2016]

M 9 Business Knigge Indien: Im Land der Gegensätze

Kai Oppel

Kai Oppel is a German freelance writer and one of the owners of a PR agency. He studied Communication Sciences and Psychology at the University of Erfurt. After successfully completing his studies, he worked as a journalist before he moved into the area of modern media and networking.

1. Imagine you are doing an internship in a company for modern media which runs the website www.business-in-india.de. On that website, information in English on India's economic potential is collected for global businesses. The editor has given you a German magazine article from the journal *Manager Magazin*. You are asked to write an article in English in which you **point out** the cultural differences to be observed when dealing with Indian companies. You should also **present** the different ideas on business communication that exist in India. Your text should have a length of about 250 words.

@ SNG-40660-006

1,2 Milliarden Menschen leben in Indien. Obwohl nach Angaben der Weltbank knapp die Hälfte von ihnen mit weniger als einem Dollar pro Tag auskommen müssen, machen gleichfalls mehr als 200 Millionen sehr wohlhabende Mittelklassekonsumenten* und schätzungsweise 30 Millionen reiche Elite-Inder das Land zu einem interessanten Markt für Import- und Exportgeschäfte.

Die westliche Welt hat dies erkannt. Indien zieht seit Jahren verstärkt die Aufmerksamkeit auf sich. Das Wirtschaftswachstum* lag zuletzt bei rund 7 Prozent. In der zwölftgrößten Volkswirtschaft* der Welt liegen enorme Chancen – und laut Experten wacht der Riese Indien trotz des rasanten Wachstums gerade erst auf.

Doch wer in Indien Erfolg im Geschäftsleben haben will, braucht harte Nerven. „Um Missverständnisse zu vermeiden, sollte man sich unbedingt mit den kulturellen Unterschieden beschäftigen", rät Manisha Bhatia, der bei der Deutsch-Indischen Handelskammer in Mumbai die Geschäftsfelder Zusammenarbeit und Geschäftsentwicklung betreut. Die Kommunikation verläuft nicht nur wegen der 400 Regionalsprachen und Idiome anders. Inder haben auch vom Leben und von Geschäftsbeziehungen* andere Vorstellungen. Die Business-Regeln sind mit jenen in Deutschland nicht zu vergleichen. Nicht zuletzt deswegen setzen immer mehr Manager bereits bei ihrer Ausbildung auf den Kulturschock* und erwerben beispielsweise ihren Master of Business Administration (MBA) in einer indischen MBA-Schmiede. [...]

Auf einen Kulturunterschied werden deutsche Geschäftspartner bereits bei der Kontaktaufnahme stoßen. Wer Indern eine E-Mail schreibt, zweifelt ganz schnell daran, dass in Indien überhaupt ein funktionierendes Internet existiert. Denn: Er wird in 99 Prozent aller Fälle keine Antwort erhalten.

[...] Egal ob beim Aufbau einer Niederlassung, ob beim Finden eines Geschäftspartners oder im täglichen Berufsalltag mit Indern: Wer in Indien höflich sein möchte und erfolgreich vorgehen will, muss zuerst in den Beziehungsaufbau* investieren. Das ist gar nicht so schwer. Man sollte einfach nie nur schriftlich vorgehen. [...]

Wer auf diese Weise mit einem Inder zusammentrifft, darf allerdings nie gleich zum Geschäftlichen kommen. Sich kennenzulernen heißt in Indien nicht nur, sich einmal gesehen zu haben. Zum Kontaktaufbau gehören nun Telefonate und Treffen. In den Telefonaten sollte man stets etwas von sich preisgeben und sich zugleich für den indischen Geschäftspartner interessieren. Als ob Adolph Freiherr Knigge seine Benimmfibel ganz für das Indiengeschäft geschrieben hätte, bemerkte er schon damals trefflich: „Interessiere Dich für andre, wenn Du willst, dass andre sich für dich interessieren sollen." Erst bei dem zweiten Treffen oder Besuch sollte man in Indien zum Kern des Geschäfts kommen.

Wichtig ist, bestehende Kontakte zu pflegen. Eine Geschäftsfreundschaft* dauert dann in der Regel mehrere Jahre an. „Weil Indern die persönliche Beziehung zu Menschen wichtig ist und nicht zu einem Unternehmen, ist es für Geschäftskontakte auch sehr schlecht, wenn in einem Unternehmen die Ansprechpartner häufig wechseln", sagt Matter. [...]

Mittelklassekonsument middle-class consumer

Wirtschaftswachstum economic growth

Volkswirtschaft national economy

Geschäftsbeziehungen business relation

Kulturschock culture shock

Beziehungsaufbau building up/establishment of relations

Geschäftsfreundschaft business relation

Missverständnis misunderstanding

Mutterunternehmen parent company

loben to praise

Unterschiede in der Klarheit der Kommunikation führen auch zwischen Indern und Deutschen immer wieder zu Missverständnissen* und ernsthaften Problemen. Mohammed Rehan erinnert sich an einen Manager, der an dieser Stelle Karl-Heinz S. genannt werden soll. S. arbeitete exakt sechs Monate als Manager in einem Pharmaunternehmen in Neu-Delhi.

Obwohl der Manager bei seinem Mutterunternehmen* in Deutschland sehr erfolgreich war, hatte er in Indien keinen Erfolg. Wenn seine Assistentin in Indien bei Anschreiben und Mails kleinere Fehler begangen hatte, wies er sie auf die Fehler hin – wie er es aus Deutschland gewohnt gewesen war. Und genau dies war sein Fehler. „Anstatt die Inderin zu loben* und sie zu bitten, die Anschreiben noch etwas zu optimieren, regte sich der Choleriker über die Fehler auf. Während deutsche Angestellte bei diesem Verhalten einfach weghören, sind Inder von der direkten Kritik entsetzt", erzählt Rehan. Die Inderin war in diesem Fall sogar derart schockiert, dass sie sich mit anderen Angestellten absprach – worauf sich das gesamte Team gegen den Chef stellte. Das Unternehmen musste darauf die Führungskraft auswechseln. [...]

Kai Oppel: „Business Knigge Indien: Im Land der Gegensätze", www.manager-magazin.de, 15.12.2008 [17.12.2015]

M 10 *Outsourced*: Working abroad in India

John Jeffcoat

John Jeffcoat is a writer and cinematographer. He is mostly known for his movie *Outsourced* which was released in 2006. Josh Hamilton and Ayesha Dharker starred as the central characters. In the movie, the character Todd (Josh Hamilton) has to train his replacement in India, after his department is outsourced to that country. *Outsourced* won a number of international awards.

1. On the basis of the promotional poster and the title of the movie, make an educated guess about the plot of *Outsourced*.

2. Watch the first scene of the movie (00:00:43 – 00:03:42) and **present** the reasons why the American company outsourced its sales-department to India.

3. **Analyse** Todd's development in India on the basis of the scenes that follow. Concentrate on his facial expressions, his overall appearance, his relationship to the Indian employees and **examine** how cinematic devices highlight these aspects.
   a) **Scene I:** Todd's arrival in India (00:03:45 – 00:05:54); (00:10:27 – 00:12:30)
   b) **Scene II:** Todd at the office (00:27:05 – 00:29:00)
   c) **Scene III:** After the Holi-Festival (00:43:48 – 00:46:44)
   d) **Scene IV:** Being flexible in the office (01:17:50 – 01:21:17)

4. Soon after his arrival, Todd is told by Asha to "learn about India". **Comment on** the importance of Todd's cultural learning process for the company as well as for his own personality.

Scene I: Todd's arrival in India (00:04:39)

Scene II: Changes in the office (00:49:25)

Scene III: Holi-Festival (00:41:28)

Scene IV: Asha's success in the office (01:22:52)

5. After having watched *Outsourced*, write a film review for your school magazine.

Zoom in: Skills

Writing a Film Review

Aim:

- In a film review, a critic looks at the positive and negative aspects of a film and evaluates it for the reader.
- The aim is to give information about the production and to judge whether it is worth watching or not.
- The style of your language largely depends on your purpose in writing the review. In general, however, it should be interesting to read and engaging.

Introduction:

- Start your review with a fascinating introduction which arouses the reader's interest.
- Use quotes, refer to a catchy scene or exploit the actor's fame in your introduction.
- Clearly state your opinion on the film.
- Point out the genre of the film and provide details on the actors.

Main part:

- Present an outline of the storyline, describing the characters as well as the action but do not spoil the ending.
- Describe whether the film is an appropriate/exciting/bad example of the genre.
- Analyse the performance of the actors as well as of the director.
- Emphasize central aspects of the film and explain your opinion on how they are elaborated.
- Discuss the use of cinematic devices and their effects in the context of the movie.

Conclusion:

- Sum up your most important points and clearly state your opinion on the film.
- Compare the film to other, similar, productions.
- Give advice to your readers on whether to watch the film or not. You may also give advice on an alternative title which you would find more exciting/interesting/thrilling/informative/engaging.

Adapted and taken from: "Bitesize: Writing for Moving Images", www.bbc.co.uk [22.01.2016]

Visions – the Future World of Work

M1 The Circle

Dave Eggers

In Dave Eggers' novel *The Circle* (2013) a young college graduate named Mae Holland has unexpectedly landed a job at The Circle, a powerful technology company that made its fortune through TruYou, a program that has removed anonymity from the Internet and allowed users to conduct all their online business using one program and one password. Mae is thrilled with the company's modernity and activity and excited about the campus that is not only covered with glass office buildings but also with drive-in movie theatres, dorms, and entertainment facilities of all sorts. Moreover, in order to make this enormous place less impersonal and corporate, each portion of the campus is named and designed after a historical era. After some time working for the company, Mae is summoned to her team leader to talk about her work ethics.

1. **Summarise** the given extract of Eggers' novel.
2. **Analyse** Dan's techniques for conducting the conversation and the way Mae responds to them.
3. Put yourself in Mae's shoes. Would you be willing to be part of the community and agree to stay at work after hours in order to socialize? **Justify** your answer.

At four thirty Dan* sent a message: "Great day so far! Meet at five?"

Mae arrived at Dan's door. He stood, guided her to a chair and closed the door. He sat behind his desk and tapped his tablet screen.

"97. 98. 98. 98. Wonderful aggregates* this week."

"Thank you," Mae said. [...]

Now Dan looked up, and probed into her eyes. "Mae, have you had a good experience so far here at the Circle?"

"Absolutely," she said.

His face brightened. "Good. Good. That's very good news. I asked you to come in just to, well, to square* that with your social behavior here and the message it's sending. And I think I might have failed to communicate everything about this job properly. So I blame myself if I haven't done that well enough."

"No. No. I know you did a good job. I'm sure you did."

"Well, thank you, Mae. I appreciate that. But what we need to talk about is the, well ... Let me put it another way. You know this isn't what you might call a clock-in, clock-out type of company. Does that make sense?"

"Oh, I know. I wouldn't ... Did I imply that I thought? ..."

"No, no. You didn't imply anything. We just haven't seen you around so much after 5 o'clock, so we wondered if you were, you know, anxious* to leave."

"No, no. Do you need me to stay later?"

Dan winced*. "No, it's not that. You handle your workload just fine. But we missed you at the Old West party last Thursday night, which was a pretty crucial team-building event, centered on a product we're all very proud of. You missed at least two newbie* events, and at the circus the other night, it looked like you couldn't wait to leave. I think you were out

Dan Mae's team leader

aggregate total score

to square to make sth. agree or combine

anxious ['æŋkʃəs] wanting very much to do sth.

to wince here: to pull a face

newbie beginner/new person

of there in 20 minutes. Those things might be understandable if your Participation Rank wasn't so low. Do you know what it is?"

Mae guessed it was in the 8,000-range. "I think so."

"You think so," Dan said, glancing at his screen. "It's 9,101. Does that sound right?" It had dropped in the last hour, since she last checked.

"It must be," Mae said.

Dan clucked and nodded. "So it's been sort of adding up and, well, we started worrying that we were somehow driving you away."

"No, no! It's nothing like that."

"O.K., let's focus on Friday at five fifteen. We had a gathering in the Old West, where your friend Annie works. It was a semi-mandatory* welcome party for a group of potential partners. You were off-campus, which really confused me. It's as if you were fleeing."

semi-mandatory half-required

Mae's mind raced. Why hadn't she gone? Where was she? She didn't know about this event. It was across campus, in the Old West – how had she missed a semi-mandatory event? The notice must have been buried deep in her third screen.

"God, I'm sorry," she said, remembering now. "At five I left campus to get some aloe at this health shop in San Vincenzo. My dad asked for this particular kind of –"

"Mae," Dan interrupted, his tone condescending*, "the company store has aloe. Our store's better stocked than some corner store, and with superior products. Ours is carefully curated."

condescending arrogant

"I'm sorry. I didn't know the company store had something like aloe."

"You went to our store and couldn't find it?"

"No, no. I didn't go to the store. I went straight to the other store. But I'm so glad to know that –"

"Let me stop you there, because you said something interesting. You said you didn't go to our store first?"

"No. Sorry. I just assumed something like that wouldn't be there, so –"

"Now listen, Mae, I should admit that I know you didn't go the store. That's one of the things I wanted to talk to you about. You haven't been in the store, not once. You – a former college athlete – haven't been to the gym, and you've barely explored the campus. I think you've used about 1 percent of our facilities."

"I'm sorry. It's just been a whirlwind so far, I guess."

"And Friday night? There was a major event then, too."

"I'm sorry. I wanted to go to the party, but I had to run home.
My dad had a seizure*. It ended up being minor, but I didn't know that until I got home."

seizure a convulsive attack, a stroke

Dan looked at his glass desk and, with a tissue, tried to remove a smudge. Satisfied, he looked up. That's very understandable. To spend time with your parents, believe me, I think that is very, very cool. I just want to emphasize the *community* aspect of this job. We see this workplace as a *community*, and every person who works here is *part* of that community. [...]"

"I know."

"Listen. It totally makes sense you'd want to spend time with your parents. They're your parents! It's totally honourable of you. Like I said: very, very cool. I'm just saying we like you a lot, too, and want to know you better. To that end, I wonder if you'd be willing to stay a few extra minutes, to talk to Josiah and Denise. I think you remember them from your orientation? They'd love to just extend the conversation we're having and go a bit deeper. Does that sound good?"

"Sure."

"You don't have to rush home or ... ?"

"No. I'm all yours."

Dave Eggers, *The Circle*, Vintage Books, New York 2013, pp. 176–180

M 2 Inside Google's Lair

Working for Google is associated with certain ups and downs as presented in this 3:41-minute BBC clip (see Webcode).

@ SNG-40660-007

1. In a book review for the *Financial Times*, journalist Lionel Shriver states that "the Circle's campus would be a parody if it weren't so close to the facilities that Google already provides for its employees." Against the backdrop of this statement and the stills below, speculate on what it is like to work for Google. Share your thoughts with a partner.

2. **Point out** how and why Google develops its ideas to improve workplaces.

3. Professor Robert Sutton compares Google to "total institutions" and labels its methods as "liberal paternalism". **Explain** what he means.

4. **Comment** on the title of the clip – do you think it is appropriate?

Stills taken from *Inside Google's Lair*

5. After having watched the clip, split the group in half and do some more research on the pros and cons of Google as an employer and **discuss** the question raised in the clip, "Google – fascinating or Orwellian workplace?", in a panel discussion.

Zoom in: Terminology

"Orwellian" is an adjective describing a situation, idea, or societal condition that author George Orwell identified as being destructive to the welfare of a free and open society. The term refers to the circumstances depicted in novels such as his *Nineteen Eighty-Four* (1949).

George Orwell

SPEAKING TEST

A speaking test as a substitute for a written exam will usually consist of two parts and you will probably take the test in pairs or in groups of three.

Part I

In Part I you must show that you can speak about a text or a visual for about ten minutes. You will be given a preparation time of thirty minutes to work on three tasks. These tasks cover the same skills as in a written test, so there will be a comprehension task and an analysis task as well as an evaluation task.

TIPS	
Make notes only. You are required to speak freely and to establish eye-contact with the interlocutors.	√
Watch your time management. You must deal with all three tasks sufficiently in ten minutes.	√
Pay attention to the task instructions. Make sure you cover all aspects of the tasks.	√
The same rules apply as in a written test. So use your own words and neutral language only in task one, apply the TEE-technique in task two, and give a balanced assessment with reference to the text in task three.	√
Your register must be formal.	√
Guide your listeners through your talk. State what you are about to do and sum up your main results at the end of each task. Make use of varied sentence connectives.	√
Speak slowly and clearly.	√

ZOOM IN: Terminology

The **Digital Revolution** (also known as the Third Industrial Revolution) refers to the advancement of technology from analogue electronic and mechanical devices to the digital technology available today. The term implies the rapid changes that have been brought about, especially since the turn of the millennium, by digital computing.

Central to this revolution is the mass production and widespread use of digital logic circuits and its derived technologies including the computer, smartphones, and the Internet. The Digital Revolution marks the beginning of the Information Era.

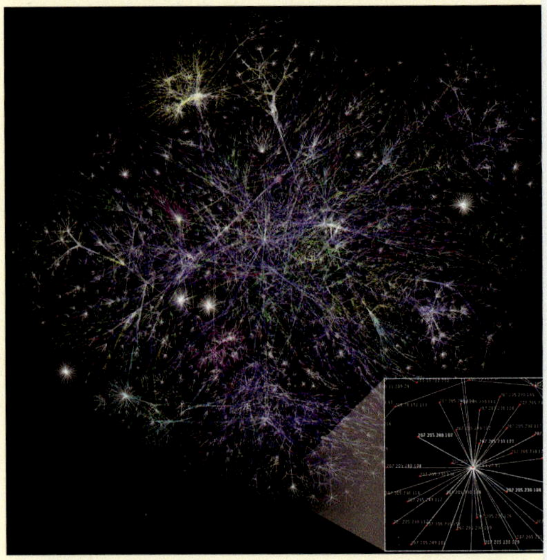

A visualization of the various routes through a portion of the Internet.

M 3a Technology Is Making Real-time Performance Monitoring Too Easy

Simon Caulkin

Not only in Dave Eggers' novel *The Circle* are employees monitored with the help of modern technology: In this article, published in the British newspaper *Financial Times* on 18 October 2015, the author criticizes the effects of the digital revolution on the contemporary world of work.

1. In the following article, Simon Caulkin connects the effects of the digital revolution to what he calls the "triumph of inhumanity". What could he mean? Discuss with a partner.
2. **Point out** the digital revolution's (potential) negative effects on the world of work.
3. **Explain** Caulkin's hypothesis that the "triumph of anti-humanity" (l. 30 f.) is the outcome of the digital revolution.
4. "We are becoming aware that the major questions regarding technology are not technical but human" (l. 44 f.). **Comment.**

[...]

Amazon, consistently voted one of the world's most admired companies, may be more systematic than others, but it is far from alone in its hard-driving* style. Studies suggest that work-related stress costs 120,000 lives and $190 [billion] a year in additional healthcare expenses in the US alone. That is not all down to one company. The harsh reality, says Professor Julian Birkinshaw of London Business School, "is that today's large business organisations are ... miserable places to spend our working lives. Fear and distrust are endemic*. Aggressive and unpleasant behaviour is condoned*."

Do not expect the pressures and insecurities to go away. It's not just that innovations made in downturns*, such as zero-hour contracts, rapidly become part of the employment landscape. The difference now is that digital technology makes real-time performance management easy and tempting for managers constantly seeking to boost performance. Big data and the "quantified self" movement* have spawned a plethora* of start-ups offering time-tracking, performance-monitoring and instant-feedback apps of the kind that Amazon urges its employees to use to comment privately on the activity of peers and supervisors. [...]

Capital markets are demanding every ounce of efficiency, they argue, and the resulting transparency and accountability will lead to greater engagement in the long run.

"In the office of the future you will always know what you are doing and how fast you are doing it," says one entrepreneur. But they don't deny that work intensification is the result. And while some people can live, or more disquietingly* collude*, with always-on surveillance (as in Dave Eggers' chilling internet-age satirical novel, *The Circle*), for others the consequence is stress and illness. One employee likened* 24/7 location-tracking software to wearing an offender's* ankle bracelet.

The other threat in these data-driven work practices is less obvious but no less insidious*. Working to multiple goals at machine-tracked tempo inevitably puts people in competition with computers. As Martin Ford warns in the *Rise of the Robots*[1], if you're working

hard-driving forceful, tough

endemic regional, native *here*: common, widespread

to condone to accept/pardon wrong behaviour

downturn period of economic decline

The Quantified Self is a movement to incorporate technology into data acquisition on aspects of a person's daily life. It is also known as *lifelogging*.

plethora large amount of sth.

disquieting causing worry

to collude to conspire

to liken to compare

offender criminal

insidious dangerous, perfidious

[1] Martin Ford, *Rise of the Robots. Technology and the Threat of a Jobless Future*, Basic Books, New York 2015

with software, you're probably training it to replace you. Automation is just the logical next step. Running this forward, the digital revolution would just supercharge trends of inequality, winner-takes-all and the hollowing out* of employment: the triumph of anti-humanity, in fact.

to hollow out *aushöhlen*

Yet these are not inevitable outcomes. For example, Carlota Perez, the socio-economic scholar, argues that, as in past waves of creative destruction, the boom-and-bust cycle* has left behind the potential for a new global "golden age" that could see digital technology driving "green" growth and sustainable global development, benefiting all humankind.

boom-and-bust cycle economic process of expansion and contraction, *Auf- und Abschwung*

But tapping* that potential won't be easy. Again, as in previous cycles, it would require bold governments and international bodies to use the crisis to reshape the conditions that caused it. [...]

to tap to make use of sth.

As it happens, they have an opportunity to face up to the challenge next month at what has become management's unofficial annual summit, the 2015 Global Peter Drucker Forum. Under the banner "Claiming our Humanity", it poses urgent questions, such as how digital technology can be deployed to improve the human condition generally [...]. It is an historic responsibility that cannot be shirked*. As Drucker remarked: "We are becoming aware that the major questions regarding technology are not technical but human." And yes, Amazon founder Jeff Bezos's contribution on that would be welcome, too.

to shirk to avoid

Simon Caulkin, "Technology Is Making Real-time Performance Monitoring Too Easy", www.ft.com, 18.10.2015 [28.12.2015]

Part II

Part II will usually be a collaborative task which you will work on with your partner(s) on a topic that requires you to keep up a conversation. You should also be prepared to answer questions asked by the interlocutor. Thus, the focus here clearly is on communicative competence and participating in discussion. Part II is of roughly the same length as Part I.

TIPS	
Do not speak for too long, but give your partner a chance to contribute to the discussion.	√
Make sure the discussion does not get stuck. You could, for example, ask what your partner's ideas are or whether he/she agrees with you or not.	√
When your partner is speaking, show that you are listening by reacting and responding appropriately. You could, for example, nod or smile as well as speak. If there is something you do not understand, ask for clarification.	√
Watch your time management. You must deal with both tasks and you must also reach a conclusion. There will be further questions the interlocutor wants to ask you, too.	√
Make use of varied phrases for expressing one's opinion instead of a repetitive "I think". Otherwise the same language rules apply as in Part I.	√

M 3b The Digital Revolution – 'Triumph of Anti-humanity' or Beginning of a 'Golden Age'?

The cartoons provided below deal with the outcome of the Digital Revolution.

1. Take turns with your partner(s) and describe the cartoons below.
2. Together, come to a conclusion: *The Digital Revolution – 'triumph of anti-humanity' or beginning of a 'golden age'?*

M 4 Niemand ist unersetzlich

Sven Astheimer

According to certain studies, artificial intelligence and robots threaten every second place of employment. *Pure panic mongering or justified fear of a world of work without employees?* The German economics journalist Sven Astheimer looks into this question and informs about the outcome of a study conducted by a group of German scholars from Mannheim.

1. What are your feelings towards humanoid robots like "Aiko Chihira" (picture)? Give reason for your thoughts.

2. **Summarise** the outcome of Frey's and Osborne's survey by considering the text (ll. 1–19) and the findings illustrated in the figures below.

@ SNG-40660-008

3. You have been talking to an American friend about the survey of Frey and Osborne as she has to give a speech in class about whether similar surveys have been conducted in other countries. Write an email to your friend in which you provide her with information about Holger Bonin's research by **outlining** the relevant content of the rest of article (ll. 20–70).

4. Together with a partner, act out a telephone conversation between you and your friend and **discuss** the question presented in the introduction.

Just like a human! The robotic humanoid "Aiko Chihira" was developed by Toshiba. Dressed in a traditional Kimono, it greets shoppers in Tokyo's Mitsukoshi department store, gives shoppers directions and holds short conversations.

Strukturwandel structural change

Ökonom economist
pauschal general

Zwar gehören der Strukturwandel* und seine Folgen für die Arbeitswelt zu den Dauerthemen von Wissenschaftlern. Doch die beiden Oxford-Forscher Carl Benedikt Frey und Michael A. Osborne wirbelten 2013 mit ihrer Studie „The Future of Employment" über die Folgen der vierten industriellen Revolution einiges durcheinander. Die beiden Ökonomen* kamen nicht nur zu dem Pauschalergebnis*, dass es für die Beschäftigten immer schwieriger werden wird, sich im „Rennen gegen die Maschinen" durchzusetzen. Anders als bei den vorangegangenen Wellen der Industrialisierung sind der Untersuchung zufolge diesmal auch nicht nur die geringqualifizierten* Beschäftigungsgruppen* vom Modernisierungsschub stark bedroht. Im 21. Jahrhundert kann sich kaum noch eine Berufsgruppe sicher sein, nicht bald schon von Maschinen ersetzt zu werden. Die These elektrisierte die Fachwelt.

Die beiden Forscher beließen es aber nicht bei Globalaussagen, sondern schätzten für mehr als 700 Berufe in den Vereinigten Staaten deren jeweilige Automatisierungswahrscheinlichkeit*. Sie unterschieden drei Gruppen: die mit niedrigem (bis 30 Prozent), die mit mittlerem (bis 70 Prozent) und die mit hohem Substitutionsrisiko* (mehr als 70 Prozent). Innerhalb der kommenden zwanzig Jahre sind laut Frey/Osborne 47 Prozent und damit fast jeder zweite beschäftigte Amerikaner einem hohen Risiko ausgesetzt, den Arbeitsplatz durch Automatisierung und Digitalisierung zu verlieren. Das wären über den Daumen gepeilt 70 Millionen Menschen. Eine gigantische Zahl.

geringqualifiziert low-qualified
Beschäftigungsgruppe occupational group

Automatisierungswahrscheinlichkeit likelihood of automation
Substitution replacement

Der Kunde entscheidet

Lassen sich die Ergebnisse auch auf andere Länder, etwa auf Deutschland, übertragen? Dieser Frage gingen etliche Folgestudien nach. Eine der profundesten Untersuchungen stammt von einer Gruppe Wissenschaftler um den Ökonomen Holger Bonin vom Zentrum für europäische Wirtschaftsforschung in Mannheim. In ihrer Expertise kommen die Forscher zu dem Schluss, dass nach der Methodik von Frey/Osborne auch in Deutschland 42 Prozent der Beschäftigten in Berufen arbeiten, die sich mit hoher Wahrscheinlichkeit innerhalb von zwei Jahrzehnten automatisieren lassen.

„Allerdings müssen unsere Ergebnisse richtig interpretiert werden", sagt Ulrich Zierahn, einer der Autoren. Vor voreiligen Schlüssen sei gewarnt. Zunächst sei zu beachten, dass Tätigkeiten untersucht wurden, nicht Berufe als Ganzes. Demnach arbeiten „nur" 12 Prozent aller Beschäftigten in den als bedroht geltenden Berufen. Grundsätzlich sei es wichtig, dass die Schätzmethodik nach Frey/Osborne „technisches Automatisierungspotential" beschreibe. Wie viel davon realisiert wird, hängt laut Zierahn von verschiedenen Einflussfaktoren ab. „Technisches Potential wird aber grundsätzlich überschätzt", sagt der Ökonom. Bedrohte Arbeitsplätze gingen nicht automatisch verloren, da viele Hürden zu überwinden seien. Dem fahrerlosen Autofahren stünden rechtliche Bedenken gegenüber. Wenn es um Pflegeroboter gehe, spielten wiederum ethische Fragen eine Rolle. Und schließlich entscheide der Kunde, was sich am Markt durchsetzt: „Will ich mich im Restaurant von einem Roboter bedienen lassen, oder gehe ich doch lieber zu einem lebendigen Kellner?"

Dass sich die Arbeitswelt durch den Technologieschub gehörig verändern wird, steht aber auch für Zierahn außer Frage. Dabei seien jedoch nicht alle Gruppen dem gleichen Druck ausgesetzt. Für Hochqualifizierte macht Zierahn nur wenig Bedrohung aus, die Beschäftigung von Geringqualifizierten habe zuletzt in vielen Ländern sogar leicht zugenommen. Häufig lohne es sich nicht, die oft als „McJobs" geschmähten Arbeitsplätze durch teure Maschinen zu ersetzen. „Die Computerisierung hat in der Vergangenheit häufig im mittleren Bereich der Qualifikation und Lohnverteilung stattgefunden", sagt er. Demnach wären Fachkräfte mit dualer Ausbildung besonders gefährdet. Die Digitalisierung der Buchhaltung ist nur ein Beispiel für diese Entwicklung. „Aber die Menschen sind wandelbar und anpassungsfähig", sagt Zierahn. Aus Sicht der Politik sei es wichtig, diese Anpassungsfähigkeit vor allem durch Weiterbildung zu unterstützen.

Berufsbilder passen sich an die technische Entwicklung an

Je höher die Qualifikation, desto anpassungsfähiger seien die Beschäftigten, sagt auch Joachim Möller. Der Direktor des staatlichen Instituts für Arbeitsmarkt- und Berufsfor-

schung weist darauf hin, dass sich Berufsbilder und Tätigkeiten permanent der technischen Entwicklung anpassen. So habe der Kaminkehrer zwar seinen Namen behalten, in Wahrheit sei er aber heute auch ein Messtechniker. Und die neue Beschäftigung, die durch den technologischen Schub entstehe, sei noch gar nicht zu quantifizieren.
Möller weist darauf hin, dass schon der Nationalökonom John Maynard Keynes auf die „technologische Arbeitslosigkeit" infolge der Industrialisierung aufmerksam gemacht habe – mit dem Zusatz, sie werde vor allem Länder treffen, die nicht an der Spitze des Fortschritts stehen. Für Deutschland sieht Möller deshalb nicht schwarz: „Wenn wir an der Spitze der Entwicklung stehen, haben wir gute Chancen." Zudem könne die Technologie künftig helfen, demographische Knappheiten zu kompensieren. In den kommenden Jahrzehnten werden dem alternden Deutschland Millionen Arbeitskräfte weniger zur Verfügung stehen.
Mit einer Antwort halten sich aber sowohl Möller als auch sein Kollege Ziehran zurück. Die Frage, ob auch die digitale Revolution wie ihre Vorgängerinnen trotz aller Verwerfungen letztlich zu mehr Beschäftigung führen wird, sei derzeit aus wissenschaftlicher Sicht einfach nicht seriös zu beantworten.

Sven Astheimer, „Niemand ist unersetzlich", www.faz.net, 06.08.2015 [28.12.2015]

bedroht threatened, endangered
ersetzbar replaceable
Wahrscheinlichkeit likelihood, probability
Versicherungsgutachter insurance consultant
Buchhalter bookkeeper
Kranführer crane driver
Zimmermann carpenter
Luftfahrtingenieur aviation engineer
Geistlicher clergyman
Kurator curator
Ernährungswissenschaftler nutritionist [njuːˈtrɪʃənɪst]

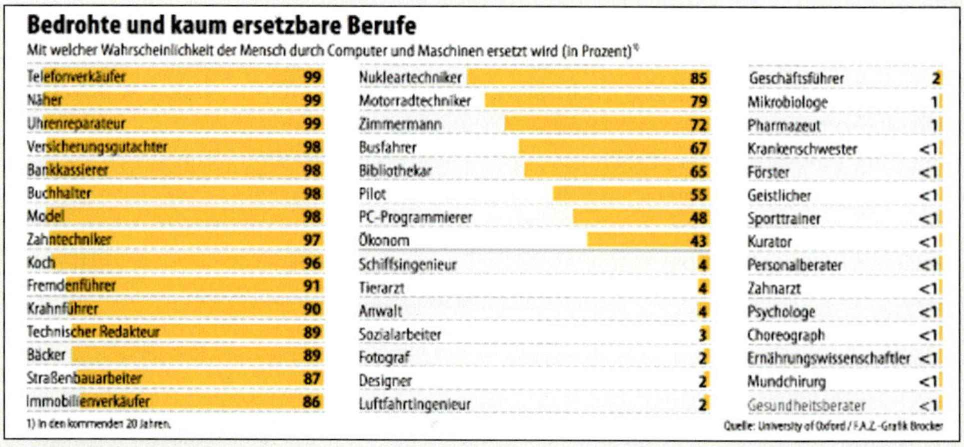

Statistics showing occupations threatened by automation and occupations that are difficult to replace by means of automation

ZOOM IN: Words in Context

The Perks and Quirks of Studying Abroad	
abroad	im Ausland
adaptability	Anpassungsfähigkeit
to attend lectures	zu Vorlesungen gehen
to be accustomed to	an etw. gewöhnt sein
to broaden	erweitern
career boosting	karrierefördernd
comfort zone	Wohlfühlzone
to cope with	mit etw. umgehen/bewältigen
cross-cultural	interkulturell/kulturübergreifend
to depart	abreisen/abfahren
diversity	Vielfalt
to embrace	jmd. umarmen/etw. annehmen
to enhance	verbessern/aufwerten
exchange student	Austauschschüler/in
to explore	erforschen
foreign students	ausländische Studierende
global education	globale/weltpolitische Bildung
to head to	sich auf etw./jmd. zu bewegen
international students' office	Auslandsamt einer Hochschule
proficiency	Fähigkeit/Leistung
rewarding	belohnend/bereichernd
to strive for	nach etw. streben
tuition fees	Studiengebühren

Gap Year – the Good, the Bad and the Ugly	
benefit	Nutzen
to blend in	sich integrieren
bucket list	eine Liste mit Dingen, die man vor dem Lebensende gemacht haben will
cultural immersion	kulturelles Eintauchen
dark tourism	Schwarzer Tourismus/Katastrophentourismus
to explore	erforschen/erkunden
to gain experience	Erfahrungen sammeln
gap year; to take a gap year	„Lückenjahr"; ein Jahr aussetzen
to go off the beaten track	abseits ausgetretener Pfade gehen
to have itchy feet	Fernweh haben
hedonism	Streben nach Freude und Genuss
humanitarian aid	humanitäre Hilfe
indigenous	eingeboren/einheimisch
to roam	umherwandern
to serve as a volunteer	einen Dienst als Freiwillige/r leisten
short-term	kurzfristig/befristet/kurze Laufzeit

touchstone	Maßstab/Prüfstein
travelogue	Reisebericht
unskilled labour	ungelernte Arbeitskräfte
vacation package	Pauschalurlaub
to volunteer	ehrenamtlich arbeiten/sich freiwillig für etw. melden
voluntourism	Voluntourismus; Mittel zwischen Urlaubsreise und Freiwilligenarbeit
International Internships and Work Experience – a Must Have?	
applicant; application	Bewerber; Bewerbung
blind application	Blindbewerbung
business etiquette	Geschäftsetiquette/Umgangsformen im Geschäftsleben
CEO (chief executive officer)	US-amerik. Bezeichnung für das geschäftsführende Vorstandsmitglied
cultural intelligence	kulturelle Intelligenz
CV (Curriculum Vitae) (BE)/résumé (AE)	Lebenslauf
empathy	Einfühlungsvermögen
entrepreneur	Unternehmer
expat	im Ausland arbeitende Person
Gen(eration) X	Generation X
Gen(eration) Y	Generation Y
globalisation	Globalisierung
GDP (gross domestic product)	BIP (Bruttoinlandsprodukt)
human resource management	Personalwesen
internship	Praktikum
job advertisement	Stellenanzeige
job board	Stellenbörse
job interview	Bewerbungsgespräch
job offer	Stellenangebot
labour market	Arbeitsmarkt
letter of application	Bewerbungsschreiben
migration crisis	Flüchtlingskrise
marketability	Marktfähigkeit
Visions – the Future World of Work	
artificial intelligence	künstliche Intelligenz
automation	Automatisierung
boom-and-bust cycle	Auf- und Abschwung
Digital Revolution	Digitale Revolution
humanoid	menschenähnlich
Information Age/Era	Informationszeitalter
panic mongering	Panikmache
paternalism	Bevormundung
structural change	Strukturwandel
substitution	Ersatz
total institution	totale Institution

ZOOM IN: Task Instructions (*Operatoren*)

Every exam you take in English consists of three tasks referring to three different performance standards (*Anforderungsbereiche, AFB*).

AFB I: Comprehension

Aspects to be considered:

- introduce your text by giving the essential information about the text at hand (author, title, text type, topic, publication, place, year, intention/target audience)
- use objective and neutral language
- use present tense and avoid contracted forms
- paraphrase (use your own words and do not use specific vocabulary which is also used in the text)
- make sure that your text is not longer than the original one
- do not state your own opinion
- do not quote

Task instruction	Definition
describe	Give a detailed account of something.
outline	Give the main features, structure or general principles of a topic, omitting minor details.
state	Specify clearly.
present	(Re-)structure and write down.
point out	Find and explain certain aspects.
summarise, write a summary	Give a concise account of the main points.

AFB II: Analysis

Aspects to be considered:

- use objective and neutral language
- use present tense and avoid contracted forms
- focus only on specific parts of the text
- stick to the appropriate terminology for analysing texts
- look at the structure of the text and the stylistic devices and explain the resulting function/effect (one very effective method for doing this is the TEE-method)

T(hesis)	E(xample)	E(xplanation)
The author makes frequent use of alliteration/enumeration/metaphor/anaphora/...	quote from the text	His/her intention is to emphasise/stress/underline ...
In addition, he/she underlines his/her point by repeatedly applying contrast ...	quote from the text	These contrasts make clear that ...

Task instruction	Definition
analyse, examine	Describe and explain in detail certain aspects and/or features of the text.
characterise	Describe and examine the way in which the character(s) is/are presented.
examine	cf. analyse
explain	Describe and define in detail.
illustrate	Use examples to explain or make clear.
interpret	Make clear the meaning of something.
compare	Point out similarities and differences.

AFB III: Evaluation

In the third task, you are either supposed to evaluate the text by giving your own opinion (Evaluation), or deal with the given information in a more creative way (Re-creation of text).

Aspects to be considered:

- use present tense and avoid contracted forms
- prove your points with reference to the text by quoting
- clearly state your personal opinion and give reasons for it
- explicitly refer to what you have dealt with in class in regard to the topic

Task instruction	Definition
comment	Clearly state your opinion on the topic and support your views with evidence.
discuss	Investigate or examine by argument; give reasons for and against.
justify	Show adequate grounds for decisions or conclusions.
contrast	Emphasise the differences between two or more things.
assess	Find and explain certain aspects.

AFB III: Evaluation: Re-creation of text

The most common assignment for task three is to transfer the information from the given text into another text type. The text type will depend on whether the original text is a fictional or non-fictional text.

Aspects to be considered:

- use language appropriate for the respective text type (e.g. letter to the editor: formal, conversation/dialogue: (in)formal)
- make a connection to the given text
- be aware of the formal requirements

Task instruction	Definition
write ...	
– a newspaper article (report comment);	Appropriate language/register (report vs. comment) Differentiation concerning – facts, opinions – being objective, personalisation/dramatisation – particular case, context
– a speech script (talk, public/formal speech, [debate] statement)	Appropriate language/register; Introduction: address of welcome/transparency of structure; Main part: structure and link to text/facts and assessment; Conclusion: e.g. summary/appeal
– a letter/e-mail (formal letter, letter to the editor; personal letter)	Appropriate language/register; author/addressee/reason for writing/form of address/complimentary close; structure: connection to topic, argumentation
– an interview	Appropriate language/register; neutral, unbiased, unemotional interviewer; introduction (topic, conversational partner); structured questioning; conversational partners act according to their role
– an interior monologue/ a conversation – an alternative ending (only advanced course)	Appropriate language/register; coherence between original and continued text

How to Mediate a Message

In a globalised world, cross-cultural and cross-linguistic encounters, whether in the world of work or while travelling the globe, are a daily occurrence. However, not everybody speaks English as well as German, which is why we need those people who can serve as **mediators** between the different languages and cultures (intercultural speakers). They help people from different countries to understand each other by **mediating** contents between speakers of different languages.

Mediation is a highly complex process that involves not only the capability of mediating between two languages but also between two cultures: one must not only understand one's own cultural background but also that of the interlocutor.

Mediation also describes the process of transforming a written or oral text from one language into another whereby the content has to be reorganized corresponding to the situation and the interlocutor's needs.

Factors that determine the content, register, style and complexity of the mediated text:
(1) the interlocutor's cultural background and the reason for interest,
(2) your personal background,
(3) your knowledge about your own as well as the interlocutor's culture,
(4) the context of your encounter and the foundation of your relationship.

Step 1: Analysing the Communicative Situation:

In general, before you perceive the message, consider the context of the communication. This information will help you to estimate which information you need to focus on and which parts of the message need further explanation. You may want to consider the following aspects:

Means	Questions to be asked
Interlocutor's background:	• Who are you communicating with? • What is his/her interest in the topic? • What does he/she know already about the topic? • What is the language background of the addressee?
Communicative situation:	• What is the context of your encounter? • What is the foundation of your relationship?
Form of Mediation:	• What text type are you going to produce? • Will you transport your message orally or as a written product? • Are you expected to produce a formal or informal 'text'/message? • How long and how detailed is your 'message' expected to be?

Step 2: Selective and Focussed Reading

With the help of the previous analysis, examine the given source. After a first reading/listening/viewing in which you focus on the gist of the message, concentrate on the relevant points for your message and select the important information. The following strategies can help you:

Means	Questions to be asked
Author's/Speaker's name and background:	• What is his/her intention? • What is his/her opinion? • What is the origin of the source?
Highlight/Note the important information in a text:	• Wh-questions ("Who?", "When?", "Where?", "What?", "Why?") • Which keywords are important for your message? • Which information is useful for understanding the background of the message? • Which details can be left out?
Point out idiomatic terms, proverbs and cultural concepts which need further explanation:	• Which persons/objects/institutions/concepts are known to you but not to the other person? • How can these culture-specific terms be explained? • Which idiomatic expressions cannot be translated and therefore have to be paraphrased (e. g. *"Fremdschämen"*, "Serendipity")? How would you paraphrase them? • Which proverbs can be tricky (e. g. *"Zwei Fliegen mit einer Klappe"* → *"Two birds, one stone"*)?
Register	• What is the register/style of the original text?

Step 3: Producing the Message

As mentioned above, the circumstances of the communicative situation determine the parameters of the mediated text. Therefore, when producing a mediated message always keep in mind why you mediate the content, to whom you mediate it, and in which situation. Bear in mind the following aspects:

- use relevant information only and leave out minor aspects
- anticipate problems concerning comprehension and add essential information where necessary (enrichment)
- paraphrase – do NOT translate word by word
- simplify where necessary
- paraphrase untranslatable words/passages

Vocabulary help

Intercultural messages can be transported both from English to German or the other way round. When you are asked to communicate a German 'text' into English, you may find the following vocabulary list useful. Keep in mind that specific genres also have a specific use of vocabulary and not all phrases are appropriate for all text types. Here is a general list of phrases for mediation tasks:

formal introduction	*written text*	• The text was published in (*year*) by (*name*) at/in (*place*) • The text deals with ... • The article focusses on ... • The essay puts an emphasis on ... • In the blog, the writer is concerned with the topic of ... • The object (information board, train time table, warning sign) presents information on ...

	oral text	• The speech (*title*) was given at/in (*place*), on (*date*) by (*name*) • The speaker talks about ... • The speaker inquires after ... • The speaker is interested in ... • The speaker presents his opinion on ... • He/She concentrates on ... in his/her speech. • In the interview/dialogue, the speakers exchange their ideas on/share their views on ... • The speakers are speaking in their role as experts on the topic of ... • The speakers were invited to talk about ... in their role as ...
transition	• This speech/video/advert was produced to underline/show/highlight ... • The author/speaker is of the opinion ... • The text reflects the need to ... • The main aim of this text is to ...	
phrases for giving additional information	• The concept of ... needs/requires some further explanation. • The term/object is specific to the German/English culture and derives from ... • This can be explained by referring to ... • This follows from the fact that ... • In Germany/Britain/USA/Australia/... this is an institution which ... • The before-mentioned term is often used when referring to ... • This is a culturally loaded term and can be understood as ...	
phrases for paraphrasing	• This is a German/English saying for ... • There is no direct equivalent for that in English but it is a proverb that highlights ... • To put it differently, ... • To put it in other words ... • Another term for it is ... • An equivalent for this term is ... • The opposite of ... is ...	